CABLES UNTANGLED

An Exploration
of Cable Knitting

by Melissa Leapman

POTTER
CRAFT

New York

Introduction

Cables, with their stitches mysteriously meandering over and under one another in beautiful patterns, were one of the main reasons I'd wanted to learn how to knit back in high school.

Like countless others, I was fascinated by their beautiful, rich texture: how cabled ropes wound their way up quintessential preppy crewnecks; how diamond cables seemed magically embossed on classic fisherman-style afghans; how incredibly, season after season, New York's fashion runways always featured exciting new takes on this time-honored knitting technique. Needless to say, they still do.

And, just like many other knitters and non-knitters, I was intimidated by cabled knitting at first. I thought that fabric that looked so intricate had to be equally difficult to make.

Here's the surprise: While cabling might look like knitting acrobatics, it's actually quite easy once you get the hang of it. Like any knitting technique (and any skill that you're just learning), it can be a bit awkward at first. Relax. Basic instructions and illustrations will show exactly what your needles should be doing, and little tips and tricks are interspersed throughout to help make the entire process easier and much more fun.

Another intimidating aspect of cables is that their patterns are often written in their own cryptic language, using a graphic layout of symbols on charts that can seem totally foreign. But these charts and symbols won't be hard to read once you understand how they work. I have even provided written translations for the first few charts just to make sure you're comfortable from the very start.

I had a great time designing the twenty-one projects for this book, and working on the Cable Stitch Pattern Dictionary was absolutely a designer's dream-come-true. The number of cable variations that are possible using just two basic stitches—knit and purl—is mind-boggling! I've included over 120 cable stitch patterns in this collection, many of which I designed specifically for this book.

I hope that as you become more and more comfortable with cables, you'll be able to use these stitch patterns in your own designs. I've even included some hints about designing with cables just to get you going.

So let's get started! We've got the whole world of cabled knitting to explore.

To Michael

Contents

Chapter 1

Basics

CABLES ONLY LOOK SCARY

While they may look difficult to knit, cables are really very easy—and fun!—to create. In this section, you'll learn the ins and outs of cabling, from selecting the appropriate tools to learning the knitting and finishing techniques required to make the projects in this book.

Take a few minutes to acquaint yourself with the language of cabling as well as the charts and symbols used in the patterns. Don't worry about memorizing anything! You can always refer to the Comprehensive Glossary of Symbols and Abbreviations on pages 18–21 as you knit. Once you've mastererd the cabling techniques presented in this book, you can begin exploring your own cable designs!

Getting Started

Believe it or not, cables add a lot of textural interest to knitted fabric with very little effort. Regardless of their complexity, all cables are made using the same simple technique: stitches exchange places within a row and are worked out of order.

TOOLS

To transpose stitches to create a cable, a stitch or group of stitches is temporarily placed onto a cable needle while the next stitch or group of stitches is worked. Many shapes of cable needles are available, from a U-shaped hook to a short, straight tool with a dip or little ridges in the middle. I, for one, prefer using a regular double-pointed knitting needle to hold stitches that I am going to shift. The slightly longer length makes it easy to hold while cabling, and since they come in sets of four or five, I never have to worry about losing one! In fact, in a pinch, I've been known to use a common bobby pin or toothpick. And there's even a way to work a cable without a cable needle at all! (But more on that later. . . .)

Cable needles are made from a variety of materials and come in many sizes. Metal ones are especially smooth, facilitating the quick transfer of stitches; this same sleek quality, however, can make them problematic for beginners. Wooden ones, on the other hand, seem to "grab" onto yarn fibers just enough to prevent unwanted slipping and sliding. They are a must if you're knitting with a particularly slippery fiber such as rayon or mercerized cotton.

Try several different types, and choose the one you like best. When selecting a cabling tool, whether it's a true cable needle or a basic double-pointed needle, be sure to pick one that's smaller in diameter than the main knitting needles you'll be using for your project. If it's too large, you'll risk stretching your stitches.

BASIC CABLING TECHNIQUES

Cables cross either to the left or to the right, depending on where you hold the stitches on the cable needle in relation to the fabric.

In some patterns, knit stitches travel over other knit stitches (as in the Left Cross and Right Cross cables); in others they move over purl stitches, creating an embossed look (as in the Traveling cables discussed on page 12).

As in most knitting, the interesting maneuvers—the cable crossings in this case—are performed on right side rows, so you can watch the patterns develop. The His/Her

Reversible Scarf on page 100 is a rare exception, since I designed it to appear the same on both sides of the fabric.

Various combinations of stitches can be crossed over others, such as one stitch over two stitches, two stitches over two other stitches, or five stitches over five stitches, for example. The possibilities are endless! Refer to your pattern for the specifics for each individual project.

CROSS CABLES
Left Cross (also known as Front Cross)

To create a cable that crosses to the left, hold the stitches on the cable needle *to the front* while knitting other stitches.

To cross two knit stitches to the left over two other knit stitches, for example, slip two stitches onto the cable needle purlwise (to avoid twisting them) and hold them *in front* of the fabric (see illustration 1).

Illustration 1

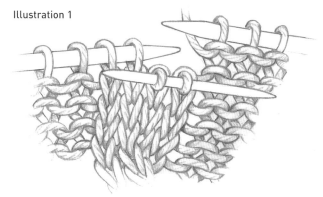

CABLING UP CLOSE

It might feel a bit awkward having three different needles in your hands, and you might worry about dropping needles—or worse, stitches. Try to relax, knowing that the stitches aren't going to unravel down to your cast-on edge and that cabling, like any new skill, becomes more comfortable and easier with practice.

If you're using a double-pointed needle as your cable needle, place it directly in front of the left-hand needle and grasp both needles with your left hand as if they were one. It'll feel more comfortable and natural there.

Now, working behind the stitches on the cable needle, knit two stitches from the main left-hand needle.

Finally, knit the two stitches that are waiting on the cable needle (see illustration 2).

Illustration 2

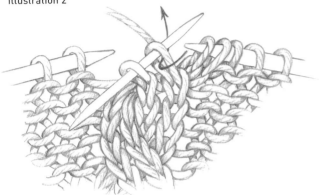

If you examine the cable, you will see that the two stitches that used to be on the right-hand side have moved to the left *in front of* the other two stitches.

Right Cross (*also known as Back Cross*)

To create a cable that crosses to the right, you'll hold the stitches on the cable needle *to the back* while knitting other stitches.

For example, to cross two knit stitches to the right over two other knit stitches, slip two stitches onto a cable needle purlwise (to avoid twisting them) and hold them *in back of the fabric*.

With the cable needle behind the work, knit the next two stitches from the main left-hand knitting needle (see illustration 3).

Illustration 3

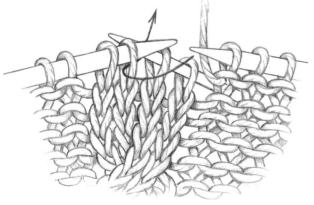

Now knit the two stitches that are waiting on the cable needle (see illustration 4).

Illustration 4

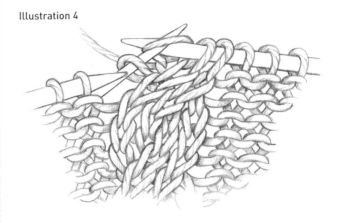

In this cable, the two stitches that used to be on the left-hand side have switched positions with the ones on the right; the ones on the right have crossed *behind* the ones on the left.

TWISTS

When a single knit stitch travels over another knit stitch, a little twist is formed. Like the Left Cross and Right Cross, this maneuver can be performed with a cable needle, holding one stitch in front of or behind the work as you knit. Or, for faster knitting, use one of the following methods.

Left Twist

Skip the first stitch on the left-hand needle, and with the right-hand needle behind the left one, knit the next stitch *in its back loop* (see illustration 5).

Illustration 5

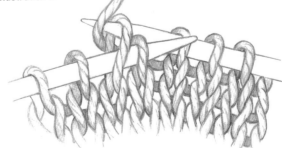

Knit the first stitch in its front loop the regular way, and then slip both stitches off the left-hand needle together (see illustration 6).

Illustration 6

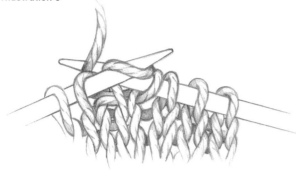

Right Twist

Knit two stitches together the regular way, but do not remove them from the left-hand needle (see illustration 7).

Illustration 7

Then, insert the point of the right-hand needle between these two stitches and knit the first stitch again *through its front loop* (see illustration 8), and then slip both stitches off the left-hand needle together.

Illustration 8

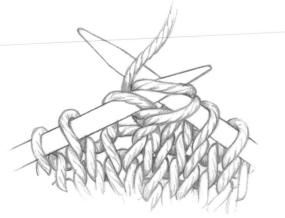

TRAVELING CABLES

Typically, Stockinette Stitch cables sit on a Reverse Stockinette Stitch background. The contrasting background adds depth to the fabric, making the cabled sections "pop." To move knit stitches to the left or to the right over purl stitches, place the stitches on the cable needle as before, but *purl* the background stitches instead of knit them.

Stitches Traveling to the Left

For two knit stitches traveling to the left over one purl stitch, for example, slip two stitches onto a cable needle purlwise and hold them *in front of* the fabric.

Purl one stitch from the main left-hand needle (see illustration 9).

Illustration 9

Then knit the two stitches that are waiting on the cable needle (see illustration 10).

Illustration 10

The two knit stitches have shifted one stitch to the left.

Stitches Traveling to the Right

For two knit stitches traveling to the right over one purl stitch, slip one stitch—the background stitch in this case—onto a cable needle purlwise and hold it *in back of* the fabric.

Knit two stitches from the main left-hand needle (see illustration 11).

Illustration 11

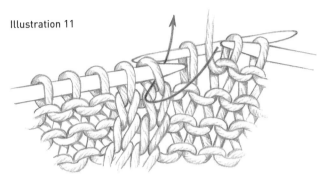

Then purl the stitch that is waiting on the cable needle (see illustration 12).

Illustration 12

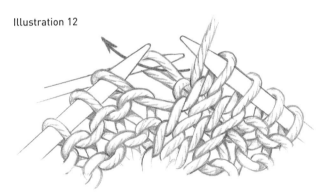

Here, the two knit stitches have shifted one stitch to the right.

CABLING UP CLOSE

Admittedly, knowing whether to knit or purl a group of stitches when working these traveling cables can be confusing, especially for beginners. To help keep things clear, remember that to move a cable toward the left, purled background stitches will be worked first, with the moving knitted stitches worked second; on the other hand, to move a cable toward the right, the knitted stitches must be worked first, with the purled background stitches worked next.

AXIS CABLES

Axis cables are comprised of three groups of stitches: two outer sections are crossed in front of (or sometimes behind) a center group of stitches that remains stationary. Like other cables, they can cross to the left or to the right. To do this maneuver, two cable needles are used.

Left Axis Cable

In a Left Axis Cable, stitches on the left- and right-hand side exchange places while moving toward the left. To cross two knit stitches to the left over two knit stitches with a single purl stitch in the center as an axis, slip two stitches onto the first cable needle purlwise and hold them *in front of* the fabric, then slip the next stitch onto the second cable needle purlwise and hold it *in back of* the fabric, then knit the next two stitches from the main left-hand needle (see illustration 13).

Illustration 13

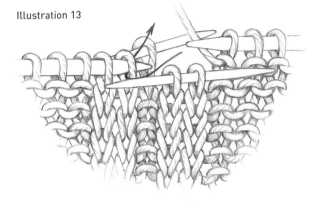

Purl the single stitch that is waiting on the second cable needle behind the work (see illustration 14).

Illustration 14

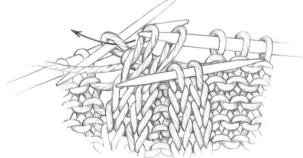

Finally, knit the two stitches that are waiting on the first cable needle in front of the work (see illustration 15).

Illustration 15

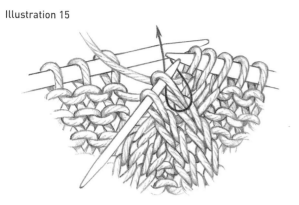

Two stitches have crossed over two other stitches toward the left, with a single purl stitch as the axis (see illustration 16).

Illustration 16

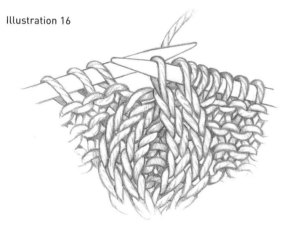

Right Axis Cable

Here, two groups of stitches are transposed while crossing over or under a center axis, moving toward the right. For example, to cross two sets of knit stitches over a single purl stitch toward the right, slip two stitches onto the first cable needle purlwise and hold them *behind* the fabric, then slip the middle axis stitch onto the second cable needle purlwise and hold it *behind* the work as well (see illustration 17).

Illustration 17

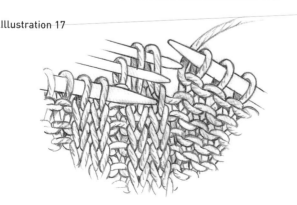

Knit two stitches from the main left-hand knitting needle (see illustration 18).

Illustration 18

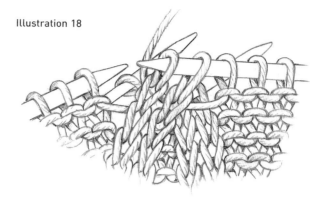

For the central axis, purl the single stitch that is waiting on the second cable needle (see illustration 19).

Illustration 19

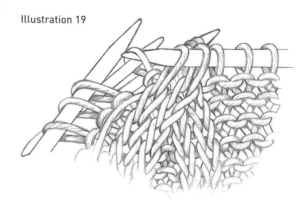

CABLING UP CLOSE

- Panel 19 on page 135 shows what happens when stitches cross *alternately* across the front and then the back of an axis. Notice how the placement of the axis stitches in front or in back makes a big difference in the cable's appearance!

- Holding all those needles—let alone keeping track of where they go—can feel cumbersome at first. Using double-pointed needles instead of regular cable needles can make the entire operation easier.

Then knit the two stitches from the remaining cable needle (see illustration 20).

Illustration 20

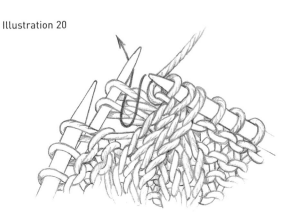

In this cable, two stitches have crossed over two other stitches toward the right, with a single purl stitch as the axis (see illustration 21).

Illustration 21

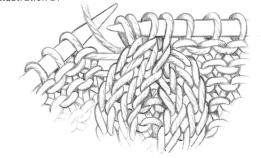

CABLING UP CLOSE

- Because of the strain of stitches moving over other stitches, cables pull the fabric in widthwise and can cause unforeseen gathers or even pleats at the top and bottom of garments. To prevent this cable splay near the cast-on edge of a project, cross your cables as soon as possible after casting on; near a bind-off edge, decrease stitches over cabled sections as you bind off, experimenting as you go. It's best to bind off immediately after a cable-crossing row.

- If you discover that you've crossed a cable in the wrong direction, don't rip down and reknit. It's easy to fix these faux pas even if you're inches beyond them! Just unravel one half of the cable down to where the mishap occurred and work the stitches back up with a crochet hook, recrossing the cable correctly.

- If your fabric contains both knit and purl stitches, be especially careful to bring the yarn *between* the needles when moving it from the back to the front and vice versa. It's easy to inadvertently carry it over the right-hand needle, causing an unwanted yarn over—and an unexpected hole in the fabric!

- For some knitters, the left-most knit stitch on cables tends to be oversized and wonky looking. It's easy to prevent this unevenness from occurring. In

fact, the hardest part is remembering to do it! The trick involves the purl stitch to the left of the offending knit stitch. Here's how to do it: on right side rows, work the offending knit stitch the way you normally would. Then when working the purl stitch immediately to its left, insert your right-hand needle into the stitch purlwise as you normally would, *but wrap the yarn around the needle in the opposite direction—* clockwise rather than counterclockwise—as you purl the stitch (see illustration below). On the next row, this stitch will present itself to you as a twisted knit stitch. Knit it *through the back loop* to untwist it.

CABLING UP CLOSE

Knitting, of course, isn't a race, so speed isn't everything unless you want to hurry and finish up one project so you can begin the next one! To make your cabling quicker, try crossing the stitches without a cable needle. The process involves setting up the stitches in their cabling position before knitting them.

For a Left Cross with two knit stitches over two other knit stitches, for example, slip all four stitches purlwise from the left-hand needle onto the right-hand needle.

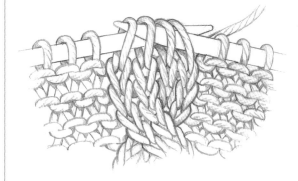

Then, with the left-hand needle in front of the right-hand needle, skip the first two stitches on the right-hand needle and insert the left-hand needle into the next two stitches on the right-hand needle from left to right.

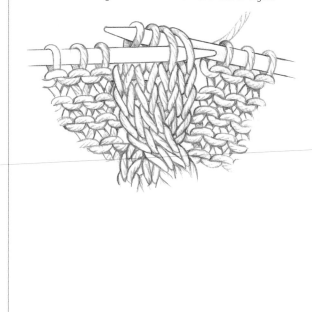

Now slip all four stitches off the right-hand needle, allowing those first two stitches to hang in midair in the back of your work.

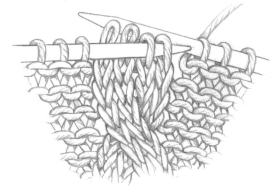

Don't forget to breathe here. And don't worry: those two stitches aren't going to go anywhere.

Rescue those two hanging stitches by placing them onto the right-hand needle from right to left.

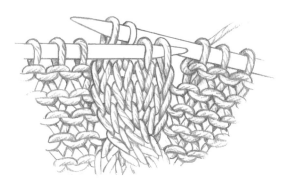

Slip the two stitches back onto the left-hand needle.

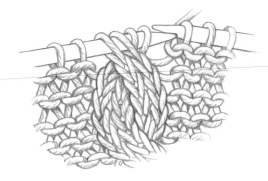

Voila! You've arranged the four stitches into their cabling position, so all you have to do is knit them in the order in which they present themselves to you on the left-hand needle.

CABLING UP CLOSE

To work a Right Cross with two stitches over two stitches without a cable needle, slip all four stitches onto the right-hand needle purlwise.

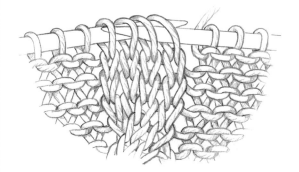

Working behind the right-hand needle, skip the first two stitches and insert the left-hand needle into the next two stitches from left to right.

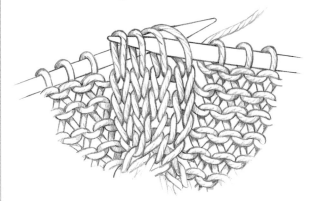

Slip all four stitches off the right-hand needle, allowing the first group of stitches to dangle in front of the work. Don't forget to breathe!

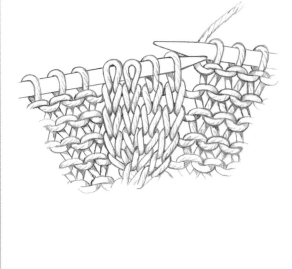

Working in front of the left-hand needle, replace those two hanging stitches back onto the right-hand needle.

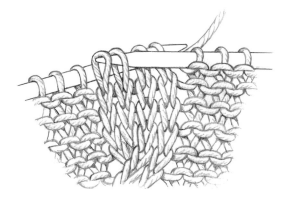

Finally, slip all four stitches back onto the left-hand needle. Knit these four stitches from the left-hand needle sequentially.

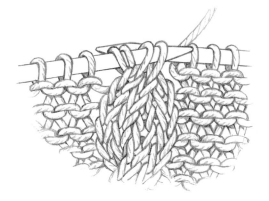

How's that for quick cabling?

Translating Knitting Charts

Knitting charts and symbols can seem like a foreign language, but they're simple to translate, and using them will make your knitting easier, faster, and much more fun.
The charted symbols are easier for the eye to pick up, or "read," than wordy instructions. Plus, they allow you to visualize what the finished fabric will look like *before* picking up your needles!

A SHORT GRAMMAR LESSON

Charts are a visual representation of knitted fabric. Each square of the grid represents one stitch, and each row of squares represents one row of stitches. The first row is at the bottom of the chart, and the last row is at the top.

Right side (RS) rows are read from right to left. The following illustration shows the order in which stitches will be knit for Row 1, a right side row, in the chart.

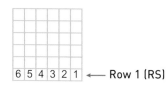

At the end of this first row, you'll flip your knitting so that the wrong side of the fabric faces you. The first stitch of a wrong side (WS) row is the same physical stitch as the last stitch of the previous right side row. Thus, wrong side rows are read from left to right as shown below.

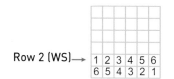

In this book, the first row knitted is a right side row, and so all right side rows are odd-numbered rows. I've numbered them on the right-hand side of each chart to keep you oriented.

CABLING UP CLOSE

If you'd like, add little arrows on the left-hand side of even-numbered rows on the charts to remind you that they are wrong side rows that you'll be reading from left to right.

When reading a chart, scan it to see what the stitch multiple is. Bold vertical lines indicate the stitch repeat. Some charts require extra stitches or half-pattern repeats on one or both sides in order to center the pattern. To read the chart below, for example, start at the lower right-hand corner, read from right to left, and work the four stitches between the two bold lines as many times as is necessary to get across your fabric, ending the row with the stitch

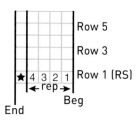

represented in this chart by the star. This stitch sits outside the stitch repeat and so is worked once per row. It is the last stitch of every right side row; since wrong side rows are read from left to right, it is the first stitch of these rows.

THE VOCABULARY LIST

Each symbol indicates the way a stitch or group of stitches will be worked; the arrangement of the symbols on the chart determines the stitch pattern. Usually, the symbols resemble the way the stitches appear once knitted. The symbol for a knit stitch, for example, is a blank box, mimicking the flat appearance of the knit stitch; the dot symbol for a purl stitch depicts the bumpy appearance of a purled stitch.

All rows are shown on the chart *as they appear on the public side of the fabric.* Therefore, symbols mean different things on right side and wrong side rows. If a symbol is used on both right and wrong side rows, the stitch key will tell you which knitting maneuver to use where.

Usually, wrong side rows are pretty simple: you just knit the knit stitches and purl the purl stitches as they present themselves to you on the knitting needle. Scan the entire chart before you begin to see if that's the case. If so, you can zip along those wrong side rows reading your knitting rather than the chart!

CABLING UP CLOSE

- Use a yellow marker to highlight the wrong side rows of charts. It'll be a visual reminder to switch the knitting maneuver on these rows.

- Enlarge your charts to make reading them easier.

- If you're a visual person, use a color key to simplify reading the symbols: choose a different color highlighting pen for each symbol in your key (see illustration at right). Instead of deciphering each symbol individually, you'll have your own useful color code!

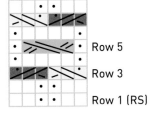

Row 5

Row 3

Row 1 (RS)

PATTERN STITCH KEY

☐ = K on RS; P on WS

• = P on RS; K on WS

= Slip 2 sts onto cn and hold in front; P1; K2 from cn

= Slip next st onto cn and hold in back; K2; P1 from cn

= Slip 2 sts onto cn and hold in front; K2; K2 from cn

- Use sticky notes or a metal board with magnetic strips to keep track of your place on the chart. Place the note or magnetic strip *above* the row being worked rather than below it. This way you can refer to the rows on the chart that are completed and see how they relate to the row you are about to knit. Compare them with your fabric; you will find that this helps in learning to "read" your knitting. Move up the note or magnetic strip as you complete each row so you're never lost!

- Place stitch markers on your knitting needles to separate each pattern repeat or panel.

- Use a row counter to keep track of where you are on the chart. If each cable panel has a different row repeat, use a separate row counter for each one.

- Study the stitch chart before working your pattern, especially if there are different cables in a panel that turn at different spots. See if the cables are related: often cables within a panel are balanced and turn on rows that are multiples of each other. For example, a narrow cable may turn every fourth row while a wider one turns every eighth row. The cable that turns at a faster rate can be a handy "row counter" for determining when to work the cables whose turns occur at longer intervals.

- Use a length of waste yarn (thinner and of a different color from your main yarn) as a "row counter" to remind you when to turn a cable. For example, if you are working a cable that turns every eight rows, run the waste yarn up the side of the first eight-row cable in the row. Flip it toward the front on the first cabled row; after working four more rows, flip it toward the back of the fabric. Work four rows, flip it forward, and work your next cable row. The waste yarn will weave in and out of the fabric every four rows, and you'll never forget to turn that cable. If you have multiple cables that turn on different rows, use multiple pieces of waste yarn. When you are finished, just pull them out!

Cables, of course, are worked over more than one stitch, so cable symbols occupy multiple adjacent squares in a chart. For the charts in this book, each line or dot within every cable symbol represents one of the stitches being crossed, so you can tell at a glance the number of stitches involved. Three lines crossing three other lines would symbolize a six-stitch cable, for instance.

Left Cross If it is a *Left Cross*, then the dominant lines in the symbol will cross toward the left, with the right-hand stitches moving *in front of* the others. When knitting the symbol, this is your clue to hold those stitches *in front of* your work.

Right Cross On the other hand, *Right Cross* Cable symbols show the left-hand stitches moving over the others toward the right. Since the right-hand stitches appear to be moving *behind* the left-hand ones, you will slip them onto your cable needle and *hold them in back*.

Cables in which stitches travel over knit stitches will have diagonal lines representing the background stitches. When stitches travel over purl stitches instead, cable symbols will have dots to represent the background stitches, as seen left. Once you get the hang of using knitting charts as visual tools it's easy!

COMPREHENSIVE GLOSSARY OF SYMBOLS

☐ = K on RS; P on WS

• = P on RS; K on WS

▨ = No stitch

Ω = K *through back loop* on RS; P *through back loop* on WS

Ω = P *through back loop* on RS; K *through back loop* on WS

I = Slip st purlwise with yarn in back on RS rows; slip st purlwise with yarn in front on WS rows

⦀ = K5 on RS; P5 on WS

B = Bobble = K into (front, back, front) of next st, turn; P1, (P1, yarn over, P1) all into next st, P1, turn; K5, turn; P2tog, P1, P2tog, turn; slip 2 sts at once knitwise, K1, p2sso

O = Yarn over

V = Increase 1 st = K into the front and then into back of st

M = M1 = Insert LH needle under the horizontal strand between two stitches from front to back and K it *through back loop*

Ψ = Central Double Increase = (Increases from 1 st to 3 sts) = K into back and then into front of indicated st and slip them off LH needle onto RH needle; insert point of LH needle behind the vertical strand that runs downward between the two sts just made and K *into the front* of it

Ⓥ = (Increases from 1 st to 3 sts) = (P, yarn over, P) into next st

Ⓥ5 = (Increases from 1 st to 5 sts) = [(P1, yarn over) twice, P1] all into next st

⋏ = K2tog on RS; P2tog on WS

⋋ = SSK on RS; SSP on WS

⋌ = P2tog

Λ = Slip 2 sts at once knitwise; K1; p2sso

△5 = (Decreases from 5 sts to 1 st) = Slip next 3 sts with yarn in back, drop yarn; *pass the second st on RH needle over the first st on RH needle; slip first st from RH needle back to LH needle; pass the second st on LH needle over the first st on LH needle; **slip first st from LH needle back to RH needle and repeat from * to ** once more; pick up yarn and K remaining st

△7 = (Decreases from 7 sts to 1 st) = Slip next 4 sts with yarn in back, drop yarn; *pass the second st on RH needle over the first st on RH needle; slip first st from RH needle back to LH needle; pass the second st on LH needle over the first st on LH needle; **slip first st from LH needle back to RH needle and repeat from * to ** twice more; pick up yarn and K remaining st

⤬ = Right Twist = Slip next st onto cn and hold in back; K1; K1 from cn OR K2tog, leaving them on LH needle; insert point of RH needle between these 2 sts and K the first one again

⤬ = Left Twist = Slip next st onto cn and hold in front; K1; K1 from cn OR skip first st and K next st *in back loop*; then K the skipped st; slip both sts off LH needle together

⤬ = Slip next st onto cn and hold in back; K1; P1 from cn

⤬ = Slip next st onto cn and hold in front; P1; K1 from cn

⤬ = Slip next st onto cn and hold in front; K next st *through back loop*; K st from cn *through back loop*

⤬ = Slip next st onto cn and hold in back; K next st *through back loop*; P1 from cn

⤬ = Slip next st onto cn and hold in front; P1; K1 from cn *through back loop*

⤬ = Slip 2 sts onto cn and hold in back; K1; K2 from cn

⤬ = Slip next st onto cn and hold in front; K2; K1 from cn

⤬ = Slip 2 sts onto cn and hold in back; K1; P2 from cn

= Slip next st onto cn and hold in front; P2; K1 from cn

= Slip third st on LH needle over the first 2 sts as if to BO; K the first st; yarn over; then K the second st

= Slip next st onto cn and hold in back; K2; K1 from cn

= Slip 2 sts onto cn and hold in front; K1; K2 from cn

RPC

= Slip next st onto cn and hold in back; K2; P1 from cn

LPC

= Slip 2 sts onto cn and hold in front; P1; K2 from cn

= Slip next st onto cn and hold in back; K2; K st from cn *through back loop*

= Slip 2 sts onto cn and hold in front; K next st *through back loop*; K2 from cn

= Slip next 2 sts onto cn and hold in back; K1; K the 2 sts from cn tog *through their back loops*

= Slip next 4 sts onto cn and wrap yarn counterclockwise 4 times around them just below the cn; K these 4 sts

= Slip 2 sts onto cn and hold in back; K2; K2 from cn

= Slip 2 sts onto cn and hold in front; K2; K2 from cn

= Slip 2 sts onto cn and hold in back; K2; P2 from cn

= Slip 2 sts onto cn and hold in front; P2; K2 from cn

= Slip 2 sts onto cn and hold in back; K2; (K1, P1) from cn

= Slip 2 sts onto cn and hold in back; K2; (P1, K1) from cn

= Slip 2 sts onto cn and hold in front; P1, K1; K2 from cn

= Slip 2 sts onto cn and hold in front; K1, P1; K2 from cn

= Slip next st onto cn and hold in back; K3; K1 from cn

= Slip 3 sts onto cn and hold in front; K1; K3 from cn

= Slip next st onto cn and hold in back; K3; P1 from cn

= Slip 3 sts onto cn and hold in front; P1; K3 from cn

= Slip 2 sts onto cn and hold in back; K3; K2 from cn

= Slip 3 sts onto cn and hold in front; K2; K3 from cn

= Slip 2 sts onto cn and hold in back; K3; P2 from cn

= Slip 3 sts onto cn and hold in front; P2; K3 from cn

= Slip 2 sts onto cn and hold in back; K3; (K1, P1) from cn

= Slip 2 sts onto cn and hold in back; K3; (P1, K1) from cn

= Slip 3 sts onto cn and hold in front; (K1, P1) from cn; K3 from cn

= Slip 3 sts onto cn and hold in front; (P1, K1) from cn; K3 from cn

= Slip 2 sts onto cn and hold in back; K3; P2tog from cn

= Slip 3 sts onto cn and hold in front; P2tog; K3 from cn

RC

= Slip 3 sts onto cn and hold in back; K3; K3 from cn

LC

= Slip 3 sts onto cn and hold in front; K3; K3 from cn

= Slip 3 sts onto cn and hold in back; K3; P3 from cn

= Slip 3 sts onto cn and hold in front; P3; K3 from cn

= Slip 3 sts onto cn and hold in back; P3; P3 from cn on RS rows; slip 3 sts onto cn and hold in back; K3; K3 from cn on WS rows

= Slip next st onto cn and hold in back; K4; K1 from cn

= Slip 4 sts onto cn and hold in front; K1; K4 from cn

= Slip next st onto cn and hold in back; K4; P1 from cn

= Slip 4 sts onto cn and hold in front; P1; K4 from cn

= Slip 4 sts onto cn and hold in back; K4; K4 from cn

= Slip 4 sts onto cn and hold in front; K4; K4 from cn

= Slip next st onto cn and hold in back; K5; K1 from cn

= Slip 5 sts onto cn and hold in front; K1; K5 from cn

= Slip 5 sts onto cn and hold in back; K5; K5 from cn

= Slip 5 sts onto cn and hold in front; K5; K5 from cn

= Slip 6 sts onto cn and hold in back; K6; K6 from cn

= Slip 2 sts onto cn #1 and hold in back; slip next st onto cn #2 and hold in back; K2; P1 from cn #2; K2 from cn #1

= Slip 2 sts onto cn #1 and hold in front; slip next st onto cn #2 and hold in back; K2; P1 from cn #2; K2 from cn #1

= Slip 2 sts onto cn #1 and hold in back; slip next 2 sts onto cn #2 and hold in back; K2; P2 from cn #2; K2 from cn #1

= Slip 2 sts onto cn #1 and hold in front; slip next 2 sts onto cn #2 and hold in back; K2; P2 from cn #2; K2 from cn #1

= Slip 2 sts onto cn #1 and hold in back; slip next 2 sts onto cn #2 and hold in back; K2; K2 from cn #2; P2 from cn #1

= Slip 2 sts onto cn #1 and hold in front; slip next 2 sts onto cn #2 and hold in front; P2; K2 from cn #2; K2 from cn #1

= Slip 3 sts onto cn #1 and hold in back; slip next 3 sts onto cn #2 and hold in back; K3; K3 from cn #2; K3 from cn #1

= Slip 3 sts onto cn #1 and hold in back; slip next 3 sts onto cn #2 and hold in front; K3; K3 from cn #2; K3 from cn #1

= Slip 3 sts onto cn #1 and hold in back; slip next st onto cn #2 and hold in back; K3; P1 from cn #2; K3 from cn #1

= Slip 3 sts onto cn #1 and hold in front; slip next st onto cn #2 and hold in back; K3; P1 from cn #2; K3 from cn #1

= Slip 4 sts onto cn #1 and hold in back; slip next st onto cn #2 and hold in back; K4; K1 from cn #2; K4 from cn #1

= Slip 4 sts onto cn #1 and hold in back; slip next 2 sts onto cn #2 and hold in back; K4; P2 from cn #2; K4 from cn #1

= Slip 4 sts onto cn #1 and hold in back; slip next 2 sts onto cn #2 and hold in back; K4; K2 from cn #2; K4 from cn #1

= Slip next 4 sts onto cn #1 and hold in front; slip next 2 sts onto cn #2 and hold in back; K4; P2 from cn #2; K4 from cn #1

= Slip 6 sts onto cn #1 and hold in back; slip next 2 sts onto cn #2 and hold in back; K6; P2 from cn #2; K6 from cn #1

ABBREVIATIONS

approx	Approximately		rnd(s)	Round(s)
beg	Begin(ning)		RS	Right side
BO	Bind off		SSK	Slip the first and second stitches one at a time knitwise, then insert the point of the left-hand needle into the fronts of these stitches and knit them together from this position
cn	Cable needle			
CO	Cast on			
cont	Continu(e)(ing)			
dec	Decreas(e)(ing)		SSP	Slip the first and second stitches one at a time knitwise, then slip them back onto the left-hand needle; insert the point of the right-hand needle *through the back loops* of the two stitches (going into the second stitch first) and purl them together as one stitch
g	Gram(s)			
inc	Increase(e)(ing)			
K	Knit			
K2tog	Knit two stitches together in their front loops as one stitch			
K3tog	Knit three stitches together in their front loops as one stitch		SSSK	Slip the first, second, and third stitches one at a time knitwise, then insert the point of the left-hand needle into the fronts of these stitches and knit them together from this position
LH	Left-hand			
M1	Insert the left-hand needle under the horizontal strand between two stitches from front to back and knit it *through the back loop*		SSSP	Slip the first, second, and third stitches one at a time knitwise, then slip them back onto the left-hand needle; insert the point of the right-hand needle *through the back loops* of the three stitches (going into the third stitch first) and purl them together as one stitch
mm	Millimeter(s)			
mult	Multiple(s)		st(s)	Stitch(es)
oz	Ounces		tog	Together
P	Purl		WS	Wrong side
patt(s)	Pattern(s)		yd	Yard(s)
p2sso	Pass two slipped stitches over other st(s)		*	Repeat instructions after asterisk or between asterisks across row or for as many times as instructed
rem	Remain(ing)			
rep	Repeat		( )	Repeat instructions within parentheses for as many times as instructed
RH	Right-hand			
			[ ]	Repeat instructions within brackets for as many times as instructed

Designing with Cables

Once you catch the cabling craze, it'll be hard to put down your knitting needles,
not to mention to stop thinking about and maybe even dreaming about cables in all their infinite variations.
It's likely you'll want to explore lots of design possibilities. Start with traditional cable patterns such as those
listed below, and then combine them, modify them, or add new elements to create your own designs! Use the
extensive "Cable Stitch Pattern Dictionary" (pages 114) for reference as you develop your designer instincts.

TRADITIONAL PATTERNS

Rope Cables

In this type of cable arrangement (see Panels 1–6, for example), usually worked on an even number of stitches, half of the stitches cross over the other half in the same direction, either left or right, and at regular intervals. Usually, though not always, these cables are crossed after the same number of rows as they have stitches (e.g., two stitches cross over two stitches every fourth row in Panel 1). Like many cables, these are most effective when placed on a Reverse Stockinette ground.

Serpentine Cables

When a cable crosses alternately to the left and then to the right at regular intervals, a curvy S-like cable is formed (see Ribs 1 and 13, for example). It's effective when worked with all knit stitches and also with knit stitches traveling over purl stitches.

Double Cables

Here, two Rope Cables are placed side by side, usually crossing in opposite directions (see Panels 10 and 11, for example). Plain knit stitches can be inserted between the two cables to create different effects (as in Panel 26).

Honeycombs

Arrange two or more Serpentine Cables next to each other and a textured honeycomb pattern develops (see Allover 3 and 5, for example).

Braids

In Braided Cables, three or more sets of stitches are intertwined at regular intervals (see Panels 14, 15, and 21, for example). They are comprised of simple Rope Cables that alternate left and right for the entire length of the cable, creating a woven effect.

Diamonds

Two symmetrical cables that travel in opposite directions to converge, cross, and then diverge will create an enclosed diamond. Fill the center with a textured pattern such as Seed Stitch—or even more cables!—for more visual interest (see Panel 28, for example). Two or more diamonds can intersect to form latticelike designs (see Panel 39 or Allover 8, for example).

COMBINING PATTERNS WITHIN A DESIGN

Cables present a wonderful opportunity for playing with design. With so many combinations of stitches and patterns possible, however, the process can be as overwhelming as it is exciting. Here are some design possibilities and suggestions to get you started.

DESIGN FUNDAMENTALS

- When arranging several different cable panels across the width of your fabric, try alternating a narrow panel with a wider one (see the woman's Cotton Raglan on page 82, for instance). It'll keep the patterns balanced while creating exciting eye movement.

- Mimic traditional Aran sweaters and position a large cable panel in the center of your design, flanked on each side by several smaller symmetrical panels, with a simple textured pattern at the edges.

- For a cohesive look to a garment, try repeating a pattern element of the body up the center of the sleeve. (See the woman's Tweed Pullover on page 68, for example.)

- Whenever possible, integrate borders and edgings into the main fabric. Well-placed increases allow cables to seem to "grow" out of ribbings. (See the woman's Turtleneck on page 86 and the Man's Tweed Pullover on page 108, for example.)

- Use mathematical formulas, such as the Golden Mean and the Fibonacci Sequence, to cut out the guesswork for proportions. (Curiously enough, even works of the Original Architect, such as sunflowers and spiraling snail shells, seem to authenticate and affirm the usefulness of these

(continued on following page)

COMBINING PATTERNS WITHIN A DESIGN

(continued from previous page)

formulas as design tools. The Golden Mean is an irrational number that's been used for centuries by architects and artists, from the ancient Egyptians to Leonardo da Vinci to Mozart, to create aesthetically pleasing works. Designers continue to use it today in determining the dimensions of such mundane objects as TV screens and credit cards. The magic number is 1.618034. Try multiplying the width of your sweater by that number to determine a desirable length, or choose cable panels whose widths are proportioned by it. Another design possibility is to use the Fibonacci Sequence: 0, 1, 1, 2, 3, 5, 8, 13, 21, etc. Here, each number in the series is the sum of its two predecessors. To use it to plan a cable project, choose panels whose widths measure the same as numbers within the mathematical sequence.

- Try placing a cable panel adjacent to its mirror image. When one zigs, the other will zag, creating visual interest and balance.

- Position three cable panels across the width of your fabric, placing the middle one at a "half drop." Here, the widest point of each cable occurs on the same row as the narrowest point of its neighbor, filling in some of the dead space between each panel. See Allover 43 on page 182 for an example of this design technique. If each panel diverges and intersects with adjacent cables, you can create beautiful, intricate patterns. See Allover 31 and 38 on pages 172 and 174, for example.

- To highlight a pretty cable panel, place it front and center with a plain stitch pattern on either side (see Woman's Simple Pullover on page 36, for example). While knitting, you'll only have to pay attention to a small section of stitches. The rest of the project will be relaxing, easy knitting!

- If you're designing a garment, place a simple textured pattern such as Seed Stitch on the side edges of each sweater piece and work all shaping over these stitches rather than on cables. It'll simplify your knitting.

- For less bulk and a summery, feminine fabric, incorporate simple lace panels between cables.

- When selecting cable panels and other stitch panels to combine in a single piece of fabric, choose ones that have the same or compatible row repeats. If, for instance, the longest cable has a 32-row repeat, others used should be 2, 4, 8, 16, 32, or possibly even 64 rows long. To knit these patterns, rechart them so they're all the same height. It'll make your knitting—and your counting!—much easier.

- If a portion of a cable is eaten away in a decrease, don't simply keep the remaining stitches in Stockinette Stitch; instead, work partial cables by crossing what's left of them at the same intervals called for in the pattern. It'll prevent long sections of solid Stockinette Stitch where it doesn't belong.

- When increasing while knitting cables (such as for a sleeve), try to work the new stitches into the pattern as soon as they accumulate, even before a full pattern multiple is added. Charting these increases on graph paper will help to plot new cable crossings.

- Use the back piece of your sweater to help determine the best neckline depth for the front. If possible, plan to begin your front neck shaping just after completing a pattern repeat and immediately after a cable crossing.

- Knit a swatch of each stitch pattern and measure its width. Use a copier to make several copies of each one and shuffle the various slips of paper until you find an arrangement you like.

- If you're computer savvy, check out some of the design-aid software that's available.

Techniques

The projects in this book assume a working knowledge of basic knitting, and each one indicates a suggested skill level: Easy, Intermediate, or Experienced. Use these designations to guide you as you browse the book and develop your skills. If a particular design excites you, let your knitterly enthusiasm inspire you to grow! This chapter provides a useful reference guide to some of the basic knitting, finishing, and embellishing skills required to make the projects in this book. Detailed instructions (often with illustrations) for a variety of techniques are included, from the specific cast-on called for in many of the patterns to different types of increases, decreases, and seams. For complete technical information on cable knitting, see "Getting Started" on page 8.

KNITTING TECHNIQUES
Cable Cast-On

The cable cast-on is, I think, the most useful, most beautiful, and easiest way to begin a piece of knitting. It's perfect when the first row worked is a right side row.

Begin by making a slipknot on your left-hand needle (see illustration 1).

Illustration 1

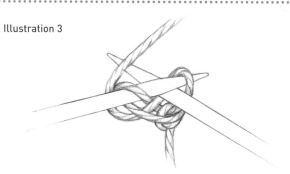

Insert the point of the right-hand needle into the loop that's sitting on the left-hand needle *knitwise*, and knit up a stitch without removing the original stitch from the left-hand needle (see illustration 2); instead, transfer the new stitch from the right-hand needle back to the left-hand one.

Illustration 2

One new stitch has been cast on.

For each successive stitch to be cast on, insert the point of the right-hand needle *between* the first two stitches on the left-hand needle to knit up a stitch (see illustration 3).

Illustration 3

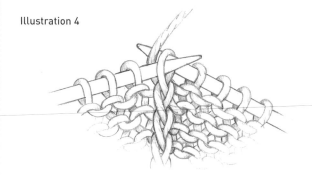

As before, do not remove the old stitch but slip the new one back onto the left-hand needle; repeat until you have cast on the required number of stitches.

Twisted Knit Stitch

Knitting a stitch through its back loop makes a twisted stitch that appears embossed on the background fabric.

To twist a knit stitch, insert the right-hand needle into the first stitch on the left-hand needle from front to back *through its back loop*, then wrap the yarn the usual way to complete the knit stitch (see illustration 4).

Illustration 4

Twisted Purl Stitch

To twist a purl stitch, insert the right-hand needle into the first stitch on the left-hand needle from back to front *through its back loop*, then wrap the yarn the usual way to complete the purl stitch (see illustration 5).

Illustration 5

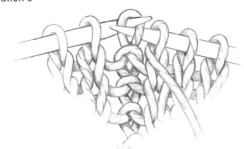

Make One Increase

This type of increase is the most invisible and perhaps the most useful one to have in your knitting repertoire.

Use the left-hand needle to scoop up the horizontal strand that's hanging between the needles *from front to back*.

Knit this strand *through its back loop*, twisting it to prevent a hole in your fabric (see illustration 6).

Illustration 6

CABLING UP CLOSE

Here, the resulting stitch leans toward the left. For its mirror image, use your left-hand needle to scoop the horizontal strand *from back to front* and then knit it *through its front loop* instead. Used in combination, left- and right-slanting stitches can create beautiful, symmetrical sleeve increases.

Three-in-One Increase

Here, three stitches are made into a single stitch. Done properly, this technique will leave no unsightly holes in your work.

Knit into the back and then the front, *in that order*, of the indicated stitch, and slip the two stitches onto the right-hand needle (see illustration 7).

Illustration 7

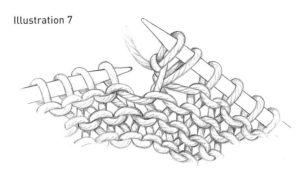

Insert the left-hand needle *from back to front* into the little vertical strand that's beneath the two stitches just made (see illustration 8).

Illustration 8

To create the third stitch of the increase, knit this vertical strand *through its front loop* (see illustration 9).

Illustration 9

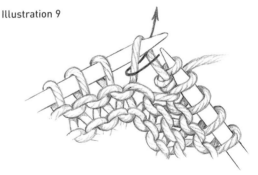

K2tog Decrease

Here's the simplest kind of decrease, and the resulting stitch slants toward the right. Just insert your right-hand needle into two stitches instead of one stitch, and knit them together as one stitch.

NOTE:
- For a K3tog, use the same method to combine three stitches into one stitch.

SSK Decrease

This decrease—known as "slip, slip, knit"—slants toward the left. It requires two steps to complete.

First, slip two stitches from the left-hand needle onto the right-hand needle *one at a time knitwise* (see illustration 10).

Illustration 10

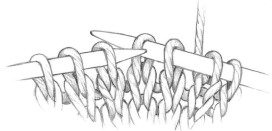

Then insert the point of the left-hand needle into the fronts of these two stitches and knit them together from this position (see illustration 11).

Illustration 11

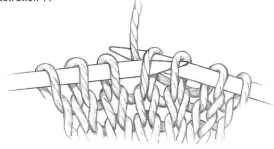

NOTE:
- An SSSK Decrease is worked the same way, but three stitches are slipped and then knitted together.

SSP Decrease

Here's a decrease that's most often used on wrong side rows; the resulting stitch slants to the left on the right side.

Slip the first and second stitches from the left-hand needle onto the right-hand needle one at a time knitwise, then slip them back onto the left-hand needle, keeping them twisted (see illustration 12).

Illustration 12

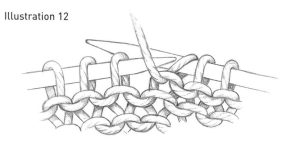

Then insert the point of the right-hand needle *through the back loops* of the two stitches (going into the second stitch first) and purl them together as one stitch (see illustration 13).

Illustration 13

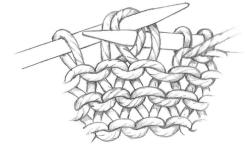

NOTE:
- An SSSP Decrease is worked the same way, but three stitches are slipped and then purled together to form a single stitch.

Five-in-One Decrease

This abrupt decrease combines five stitches into one stitch. The method involves manipulating stitches without knitting them, passing each stitch over a center stitch one by one in alternate directions until only the one middle stitch remains.

Drop the yarn behind the work, and slip three stitches from the left-hand needle onto the right-hand needle.

*Pass the second stitch on the right-hand needle over the first stitch as if you're binding it off (see illustration 14).

Illustration 14

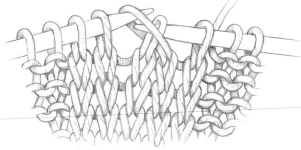

Slip this stitch from the right-hand needle back onto the left-hand needle, and pass the second stitch on the left-hand needle over the first stitch as if you're binding it off* (see illustration 15).

Illustration 15

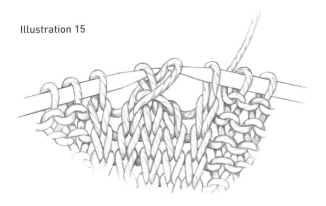

Slip this stitch from the left-hand needle back onto the right-hand needle and repeat between the two asterisks once more.

Finally, purl this remaining stitch.

NOTE:
• A Seven-in-One Decrease is worked the same way, except four stitches are slipped to begin with, and the maneuver between the asterisks above is repeated two times, combining seven stitches into one stitch.

Bobbles
Knitted bobbles add unexpected texture to cabled fabrics. Multiple increases are worked into a single stitch, a few rows are worked, then multiple decreases are worked in order to return to the original stitch count. Here's the method I suggest for neat and perky bobbles.

Knit into the (front, back, front) of a single stitch, turn; *working into these same three stitches*, purl next stitch, then (purl, yarn over, purl) *all into the next stitch*, then purl next stitch, turn; knit the five stitches, turn; decrease from five stitches down to three stitches as follows: purl next two stitches together, purl next stitch, then purl next two stitches together, turn. Finally, decrease from three stitches down to one stitch as follows: slip two stitches at once knitwise, knit the next stitch, then pass the two slipped stitches from the right-hand needle over the last knit stitch as if you're binding them off.

Fair-Isle Technique
(also called "stranded" technique)
In this type of knitting, two colors are used in the same row, with the one not in use carried loosely behind the work on the wrong side until it's needed again. Be especially careful not to pull these floats too tautly as you knit in order to prevent puckering of the fabric.

The two yarns should always maintain the same relationship to each other on all rows; in other words, they should *never*

twist, nor should one ever be below the other on one row and above the other in the following row. Otherwise, the reversal of positions will be evident on the public side of the fabric.

One advanced way of working fair-isle is to hold one yarn in the left hand (worked in "Continental" fashion, or picked) and the other in the right (worked "English" style, using the throwing motion). This not only ensures that the yarns are always in the correct position and untwisted, but also helps the knitter maintain an even tension.

EXTRA EMBELLISHMENTS
Basic Fringe
Fringe can stabilize the edge of a piece of knitting and easily adds a decorative touch!

First, cut a piece of cardboard to your desired fringe length.

Wind the yarn *loosely* around the cardboard the number of times specified in the pattern, and then cut across one end.

With the right side of your project facing you, fold several strands of fringe in half and use a crochet hook to loop them onto the edge of your project.

Pull the loose ends through the folded loop (see illustration 1).

Illustration 1

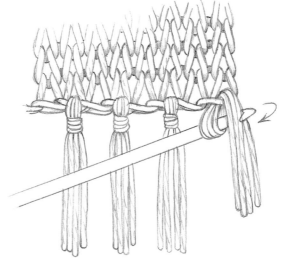

Trim the fringe evenly.

Knotted Fringe

Here, tufts of fringe are knotted together for a fancy effect. Be sure your fringe is extra long to begin with in order to accommodate the additional knotting.

Begin by attaching basic fringe along the edge of your piece. Working from right to left, knot half of the strands from the first tuft to half of the strands from the second tuft, approximately ¾" down from the first row of knots.

Continue across, knotting half of each tuft to half of the next one (see illustration 2).

Illustration 2

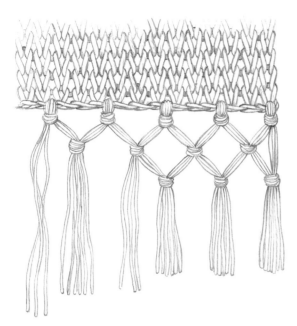

Twisted Cord

Cut yarn approximately three times the desired finished length of your twisted cord.

With someone holding one end, or with one end tied to a doorknob, twist the strands clockwise until the yarn is taut and begins to curl.

Fold in half, allow the cords to twist back on each other, and secure the two ends together to prevent unraveling.

FINISHING TECHNIQUES
Blocking

Prior to seaming your knitted pieces, take the time to block them into shape. You'll be surprised at how this simple process can improve the appearance of your projects and even out your most unruly stitches! To do so, follow the laundering instructions on the yarn label, then use rustless pins to shape the damp fabric to your desired measurements and allow to dry. Or gently steam them into shape by placing a damp cloth over them, and then carefully waft a hot steam iron just above the fabric. Don't actually touch the iron to the fabric or you'll risk flattening it.

Hiding Yarn Tails

Use a pointed-end yarn needle to make short running stitches on the wrong side of your fabric in a diagonal line for about 1" or so, piercing the yarn strands that comprise the stitches of your fabric. Then work back again to where you began, working alongside your previous running stitches. Finally, to secure the tail, work a stitch or two and actually pierce the stitches you just created. Be sure to work each tail individually, in opposite diagonal directions, and you will secure your yarn ends while keeping the public side of your fabric beautiful.

Mattress Stitch Seam
(also called "invisible weaving")

First, lay your pieces flat, with the public sides of the fabric facing you, matching patterns and stripes, if applicable. Thread a blunt-end yarn needle with your sewing yarn, then bring the needle up *from back to front* through the left-hand piece of fabric, going in one stitch from the edge, leaving a 6" tail.

Bring the yarn up and through the corresponding spot on the right-hand piece to secure the lower edges.

Insert the needle *from front to back* into the same spot on the left-hand piece where the needle emerged last time, and bring it up through the corresponding place of the next row of knitting.

Insert the needle *from front to back* into the same spot on the right-hand piece where the needle emerged last time, and bring it up through the corresponding place of the next row of knitting.

Repeat the last two steps until you've sewn a couple of inches, then pull firmly on the sewing yarn to bring the pieces of fabric together, allowing the two stitches on the edges of each piece to roll to the wrong side.

Continue this way until your seam is complete (see illustration 1).

Illustration 1

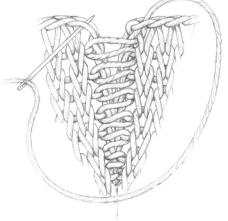

Sweater Assembly

Sweater pieces fit together like a jigsaw puzzle, with the type of armhole determining how the front, back, and sleeves interlock.

Refer to the illustrations at right when assembling sweaters.

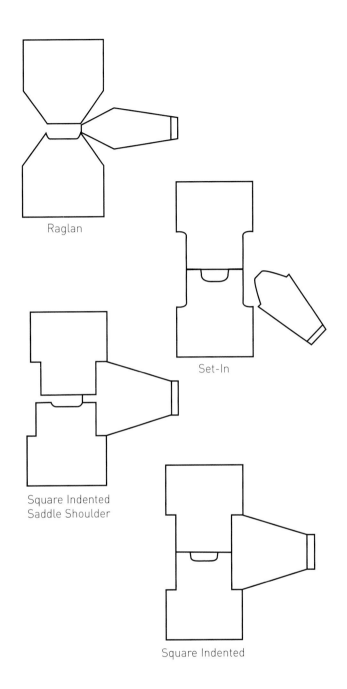

Raglan

Set-In

Square Indented
Saddle Shoulder

Square Indented

Chapter 2

Just go for it!

·····························

SIMPLE PROJECTS FOR CABLING BEGINNERS

Are you new to cable knitting? You're in the right place, and you're not alone! I have designed these first few projects with the novice in mind. In the hat-and-scarf-set pattern—and even in the sweater pattern—shaping is kept to a minimum. All you'll need to focus on is learning and practicing basic cable maneuvers.

If it's deciphering charts that has kept you away from cabling, relax! Each cable stitch pattern in this section is offered in both text and chart form. Before long, you'll become a chart-reading pro!

Simple Hat and Scarf Set

In these first few patterns, I've included written-out instructions to help with chart translation.
If you're new to cabling, start with this set of winter warmers knit out of yummy, soft cashmere.
You'll enjoy making—and wearing!—the finished pieces.

Skill Level
Easy

Sizes
Average Woman's (Man's) size. Instructions are for woman's size, with changes for man's size noted in parentheses as necessary.

Finished Measurements
Hat circumference: 19 (20½)" Scarf: 6 x 61"

Materials
- Classic Elite Yarns's Lavish (4-worsted weight; 100% cashmere; each approx 1¾ oz/50 g and 125 yd/114 m), 5 hanks in #92559 Precious Pink [1½ balls for hat; 3½ balls for scarf]
- One pair of size 7 (4.5 mm) knitting needles or size needed to obtain gauge
- One size 7 (4.5 mm) circular knitting needle, 16" long, or size needed to obtain gauge
- One set of size 7 (4.5 mm) double-pointed knitting needles or size needed to obtain gauge
- One cable needle
- One stitch marker
- One blunt-end yarn needle

Gauge
In Braided Cable Rib Patt, 28 sts and 28 rows = 4".
To save time, take time to check gauge.

Stitch Patterns
K2 P2 Rib Pattern *(mult 4 sts)*
Patt Rnd (RS): *K2, P2. Repeat from * around.
Repeat Patt Rnd for patt.

Hat Braided Cable Rib Pattern *(mult 12 sts)*
See chart at right or refer to written out translation.

Scarf Braided Cable Rib Pattern *(mult 12 + 6 sts)*
See chart on page 34 or refer to written out translation.

NOTES
- **Constructionwise,** the hat is made in the round; the scarf is made flat in rows.
- **When making the hat,** change to double-pointed needles when there are no longer enough stitches remaining to knit comfortably with the circular needle.

HAT
With circular needle, CO 88 (96) sts. Join, being careful not to twist sts. Place marker to indicate beg of rnd.

Beg K2 P2 Rib Patt, and work even until piece measures approx 4" from beg.

Next Rnd (Increase Rnd): *K2, P2, (M1, knit into front and back of next st) two times, P2. Repeat from * around—132 (144) sts.

Beg Hat Braided Cable Rib Patt, and work even until piece measures approx 8" from beg, ending after Rnd 4 of patt.

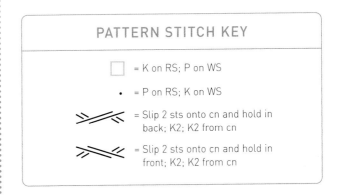

PATTERN STITCH KEY

☐ = K on RS; P on WS

• = P on RS; K on WS

= Slip 2 sts onto cn and hold in back; K2; K2 from cn

= Slip 2 sts onto cn and hold in front; K2; K2 from cn

HAT BRAIDED CABLE RIB PATTERN

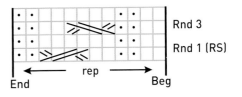

Rnd 3
Rnd 1 (RS)
End   rep   Beg

TRANSLATION FOR HAT BRAIDED CABLE RIB PATTERN CHART

Hat Braided Cable Rib Pattern *(mult 12 sts)*
Rnd 1 (RS): *K2, P2, K2, slip 2 sts onto cn and hold in back, K2, K2 from cn, P2. Repeat from * around.
Rnd 2: *K2, P2, K6, P2. Repeat from * around.
Rnd 3: *K2, P2, slip 2 sts onto cn and hold in front, K2, K2 from cn, K2, P2. Repeat from * around.
Rnd 4: As Rnd 2.
Repeat Rnds 1-4 for patt.

Decrease for Crown

See Hat Crown Pattern chart below or refer to written out translation.

HAT CROWN PATTERN

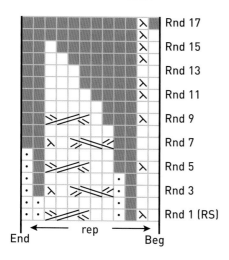

Rnd 17
Rnd 15
Rnd 13
Rnd 11
Rnd 9
Rnd 7
Rnd 5
Rnd 3
Rnd 1 (RS)

End   rep   Beg

TRANSLATION FOR HAT CROWN PATTERN CHART

Rnd 1: *K1, SSK, P1, K2, slip 2 sts onto cn and hold in back, K2, K2 from cn, P2. Repeat from * around—121 (132) sts rem.

Rnd 2: *K2, P1, K6, P2. Repeat from * around—121 (132) sts.

Rnd 3: *K2, P1, slip 2 sts onto cn and hold in front, K2, K2 from cn, K1, SSK, P1. Repeat from * around—110 (120) sts rem.

Rnd 4: *K2, P1, K6, P1. Repeat from * around—110 (120) sts.

Rnd 5: *K1, SSK, K2, slip 2 sts onto cn and hold in back, K2, K2 from cn, P1. Repeat from * around—99 (108) sts rem.

Rnd 6: *K8, P1. Repeat from * around—99 (108) sts.

Rnd 7: *K2, slip 2 sts onto cn and hold in front, K2, K2 from cn, K1, SSK. Repeat from * around—88 (96) sts rem.

Rnd 8: Knit around—88 (96) sts.

Rnd 9: *K1, SSK, K1, slip 2 sts onto cn and hold in back, K2, K2 from cn. Repeat from * around—77 (84) sts rem.

Rnd 10: Knit around—77 (84) sts.

Rnd 11: K1, *SSK, K5. Repeat from * around, ending rnd with SSK, K4—66 (72) sts rem.

Rnd 12: K1, *SSK, K4. Repeat from * around, ending rnd with SSK, K3—55 (60) sts rem.

Rnd 13: Knit around—55 (60) sts.

(continued in next column)

TRANSLATION FOR HAT CROWN PATTERN CHART

(continued from previous column)

Rnd 14: K1, *SSK, K3. Repeat from * around, ending rnd with SSK, K2—44 (48) sts rem.

Rnd 15: K1, *SSK, K2. Repeat from * around, ending rnd with SSK, K1—33 (36) sts rem.

Rnd 16: *K1, SSK. Repeat from * around—22 (24) sts rem.

Rnd 17: *SSK. Repeat from * around—11 (12) sts rem.

Finishing

When Rnd 17 is completed, cut yarn, leaving long tail.

Then, using blunt-end yarn needle, thread tail through rem 11 (12) sts, draw up tightly, and fasten securely.

SCARF

With straight needles, CO 42 sts.

Beg Scarf Braided Cable Rib Patt, and work even until piece measures approx 61" from beg.

Finishing

BO *loosely* in patt.

PATTERN STITCH KEY

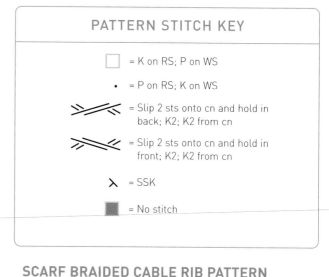

□ = K on RS; P on WS

• = P on RS; K on WS

= Slip 2 sts onto cn and hold in back; K2; K2 from cn

= Slip 2 sts onto cn and hold in front; K2; K2 from cn

⅄ = SSK

▓ = No stitch

SCARF BRAIDED CABLE RIB PATTERN

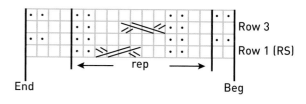

Row 3
Row 1 (RS)

End   rep   Beg

TRANSLATION FOR SCARF BRAIDED CABLE RIB PATTERN CHART

Scarf Braided Cable Rib Pattern *(mult 12 + 6 sts)*
Row 1 (RS): K4, *P2, K2, slip 2 sts onto cn and hold in back, K2, K2 from cn, P2, K2. Repeat from * across, ending row with K2.
Row 2: K2, *P2, K2, P6, K2. Repeat from * across, ending row with P2, K2.

Row 3: K4, *P2, slip 2 sts onto cn and hold in front, K2, K2 from cn, K2, P2, K2. Repeat from * across, ending row with K2.
Row 4: As Row 2.
Repeat Rows 1-4 for patt.

Woman's Simple Pullover

A traditional Rope Cable winds its way up the center of this sweater.
Worked in a lofty alpaca-blend yarn, it'll be easy to knit and comfy to wear.

Skill Level
Easy

Sizes
Small (Medium, Large, 1X). Instructions are for smallest size, with changes for other sizes noted in parentheses as necessary.

Finished Measurements
Bust: 38½ (46, 53, 60)"
Total length: 27¾ (28, 28½, 29)"

Materials
- JCA/Reynolds's Blizzard (6-super bulky weight; 65% alpaca/35% acrylic; each approx 3½ oz/100 g and 66 yd/60 m), 11 (13, 15, 17) balls in #612 Ice Blue
- One pair *each* of sizes 13 and 15 (9 and 10 mm) knitting needles or size needed to obtain gauge
- One cable needle
- One stitch holder
- One blunt-end yarn needle

Gauge
In Stockinette St Patt with larger needles, 9 sts and 13 rows = 4". **To save time, take time to check gauge.**

Stitch Patterns
K2 P2 Rib Pattern *(mult of 4 + 2 sts)*
Row 1 (RS): *K2, P2. Repeat from * across, ending row with K2.
Row 2: *P2, K2. Repeat from * across, ending row with P2.
Repeat Rows 1 and 2 for patt.

Stockinette Stitch Pattern *(any number of sts)*
Row 1 (RS): Knit across.
Row 2: Purl across.
Repeat Rows 1 and 2 for patt.

Rope Cable Pattern *(12-st panel)*
See chart on page 39 or refer to written out translation on page 39.

NOTES
- **For fully-fashioned decreases:** On RS rows, K3, SSK, work across in patt as established until 5 sts rem, ending row with K2tog, K3; on WS rows, P3, P2tog, work across in patt as established until 5 sts rem in row, ending row with SSP, P3.
- **For ease in finishing,** instructions include one selvedge st each side; these sts are not reflected in final measurements.
- **For sweater assembly,** refer to the illustration for set-in construction on page 29.

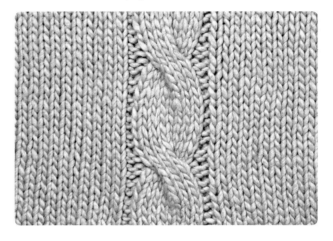

Back
With smaller needles, CO 48 (56, 64, 72) sts.

Set Up Border Patts
Row 1 (RS): Work Row 1 of K2 P2 Rib Patt over first 18 (22, 26, 30) sts, P2, K8, P2, work Row 1 of K2 P2 Rib Patt across to end row.

Row 2: Work Row 2 of K2 P2 Rib Patt over first 18 (22, 26, 30) sts, K2, P8, K2, work Row 2 of K2 P2 Rib Patt across to end row.

Repeat last two rows once more.

Change to larger needles.

Set Up Main Patts
Row 1 (RS): K1, M1, work Row 1 of Stockinette St Patt over next 17 (21, 25, 29) sts, place marker, work Row 1 of Rope Cable Patt over next 12 sts, place marker, work Row 1 of Stockinette St Patt over next 17 (21, 25, 29) sts, M1, K1—50 (58, 66, 74) sts.

Cont even in patts as established until piece measures approx 18" from beg, ending after WS row.

Shape Armholes

BO 2 (3, 5, 6) sts at beg of next two rows—46 (52, 56, 62) sts rem.

Work fully-fashioned decreases each side every row 5 (7, 10, 12) times, then every other row 2 (2, 1, 1) times—32 (34, 34, 36) sts rem.

Cont even in patt until piece measures approx 25¾ (26, 26½, 27)" from beg, ending after WS row.

Shape Shoulders

BO 2 (2, 2, 3) sts at beg of next four rows.

BO 2 (3, 3, 2) sts at beg of next two rows—20 sts rem.

BO in patt.

Front

Work same as Back until piece measures approx 24¾ (25, 25½, 26)" from beg, ending after WS row.

Shape Neck

Next Row (RS): Work across first 10 (11, 11, 12) sts; slip middle 12 sts onto holder; join second ball of yarn and work to end row. Make a note about which row of Rope Cable Patt you are on.

Work both sides at once with separate balls of yarn, and dec 1 st each neck edge every row four times—6 (7, 7, 8) sts rem each side.

Cont even, if necessary, until piece measures same as Back to shoulders.

Shape Shoulders

Work both sides at once with separate balls of yarn, complete same as for Back.

Sleeves

With smaller needles, CO 42 (42, 46, 46) sts.

Beg K2 P2 Rib Patt, and work even for four rows.

Change to larger needles, beg Stockinette St Patt, and work fully-fashioned decreases each side on next row and then every twelfth row 0 (0, 3, 0) times, every sixteenth row 2 (0, 0, 2) times, then every twenty-fourth row 0 (1, 0, 0) times—36 (38, 38, 40) sts.

Cont even until piece measures approx 18" from beg, ending after WS row.

Shape Cap

BO 2 (3, 5, 6) sts at beg of next two rows—32 (32, 28, 28) sts rem.

Work fully-fashioned decreases each side every other row 1 (3, 7, 8) times, then every row 9 (7, 1, 0) times—12 sts rem.

BO 2 sts at beg of next six rows—4 sts rem.

BO.

Finishing

Block pieces (see "Blocking") to measurements.

Sew left shoulder seam.

Neckband

With WS facing and smaller needles, pick up and knit 46 sts along neckline, including 12 sts from front neck holder.

Beg K2 P2 Rib Patt, cont Rope Cable Patt as established over 12 front neck sts, until neckband measures approx 4" from beg, ending after Row 3 of Rope Cable Patt.

BO *loosely* in patt.

Sew right shoulder seam, including side of neckband.

Set in Sleeves.

Sew sleeve and side seams.

CABLING UP CLOSE

It's important to keep track of which row you're on so you know when it's time to turn the cable. Keep a piece of scratch paper handy as you knit and tick off each row as you go. Or, if your waistline permits, put a pile of twelve tiny candies or nuts on the table next to you. Eat one for each row you complete. When you've eaten all of them, it's cable-crossing time!

PATTERN STITCH KEY

- • = P on RS; K on WS

- ☐ = K on RS; P on WS

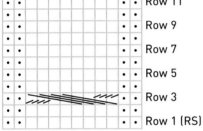 = Slip 4 sts onto cn and hold in front; K4; K4 from cn

ROPE CABLE PATTERN

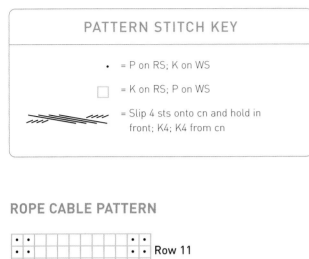

Row 11

Row 9

Row 7

Row 5

Row 3

Row 1 (RS)

TRANSLATION FOR CABLE CHART

Rope Cable Pattern *(12-st panel)*
Row 1 (RS): P2, K8, P2.
Row 2 and all WS rows: K2, P8, K2.
Row 3: P2, slip 4 sts onto cn and hold in front, K4, K4 from cn, P2.
Rows 5, 7, 9, and 11: As Row 1.
Row 12: As Row 2.
Repeat Rows 1-12 for patt.

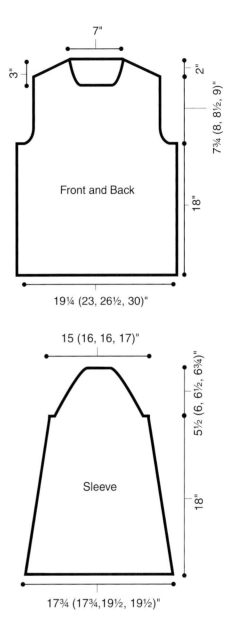

7"

3"

2"

7¾ (8, 8½, 9)"

Front and Back

18"

19¼ (23, 26½, 30)"

15 (16, 16, 17)"

5½ (6, 6½, 6¾)"

Sleeve

18"

17¾ (17¾,19½, 19½)"

Chapter 3

Cozy Cables to Cuddle Up With

ACCENTS FOR THE HOME

Cables aren't just for clothing and fashion accessories. Here are seven beautiful projects for your home that will showcase your cabling skills. From afghans to accent pillows to throw rugs, these projects will warm up any room, transforming it into a cozy haven.

Need to freshen up that sofa? Knit a colorful throw pillow. Want your comfortable reading nook to be just a little more inviting? Make a cuddly handmade afghan. And to really wow your guests, knit the Sampler Afghan on page 58. It is truly a showstopper!

Perpendicular Squares Afghan

Master one cable chart and you can knit this striking throw!
You create its visual interest by turning each adjacent block on its side. So easy!

Skill Level
Easy

Size
One size

Finished Measurements
Approx 53 x 62"

Materials
- Paton's Classic Wool (4-worsted weight; 100% wool; each approx 3½ oz/100 g and 223 yd/204 m), 18 balls in #208 Burgundy
- One pair of size 7 (4.5 mm) knitting needles or size needed to obtain gauge
- One size 7 (4.5 mm) circular knitting needle, 29" or longer
- One cable needle
- One blunt-end yarn needle

Gauge
In patt, each Afghan Square measures approx 8¾" square.
To save time, take time to check gauge.

NOTE
- **For a coordinating throw pillow,** K eight afghan squares. Use four for the front and four for the back, alternating the direction of the cables. Sew three sides together, insert a 16"-square pillow form, and then sew the final seam.

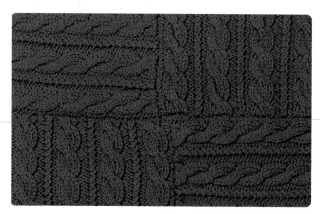

Stitch Pattern
Alternating Cables Pattern *(mult 12 + 12 sts)*
See chart on page 43.

Afghan Square
(Make forty-two squares)
CO 60 sts.

Beg Alternating Cables Patt.

Repeat Rows 1-8 of patt seven times total.

BO *loosely* in patt.

Finishing
Block (see "Blocking" on page 28) each Afghan Square to measurements.

With RS facing, sew Afghan Squares tog into six strips of seven Squares each, alternating direction of cables as seen in photograph.

Sew strips tog.

Edging
With RS facing and circular knitting needle, pick up and knit 330 sts along one short edge of afghan.

Next Row (WS): Knit across.

Next Row: Purl across.

Next Row: BO *loosely* knitwise.

Repeat for other short edge.

With RS facing and circular knitting needle, pick up and knit 385 sts along one long edge of afghan.

Complete same as short side.

Repeat for other long edge.

PATTERN STITCH KEY

☐ = K on RS; P on WS

• = P on RS; K on WS

⟩⟨ = Right Twist = Slip next st onto cn and hold in back; K1; K1 from cn OR K2tog, leaving them on LH needle; insert point of RH needle between these 2 sts and K the first one again

= Slip 3 sts onto cn and hold in front; K3; K3 from cn

ALTERNATING CABLES PATTERN

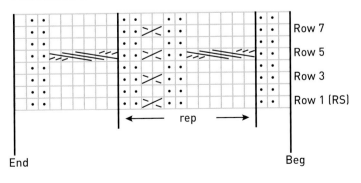

Row 7
Row 5
Row 3
Row 1 (RS)

← rep →

End   Beg

Entwined Cables Pillow

Don't let the size of the cable chart in this pattern fool you: the stitches travel in a logical fashion, and I'll bet that before long you'll find yourself not having to refer to it at all!

Skill Level
Intermediate

Size
One size

Finished Measurements
Approx 18 x 18"

Materials
- Plymouth Yarn Company's Galway (4-worsted weight; 100% wool; each approx 3½ oz/100 g and 210 yd/192 m), 6 balls in #127 Celadon
- One pair of size 8 (5 mm) knitting needles or size needed to obtain gauge
- One cable needle
- One blunt-end yarn needle
- One 18" pillow form

Gauge
In Entwined Cables Patt, 27 sts and 28 rows = 4".
To save time, take time to check gauge.

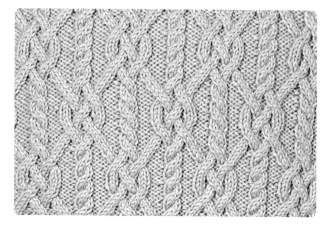

Stitch Pattern
Entwined Cables Pattern *(mult 22 + 18 sts)*
See chart on page 45.

NOTE
- **When attaching the twisted cord around the pillow,** don't simply tie the ends together. Instead, wind yarn around the abutted ends and then sew through the winding yarn and ends of the cord, piercing the yarn to keep it stable. Once completed, it'll look like the finished ends of a length of rope!

Back
CO 128 sts.

Beg Entwined Cables Patt.

Work through the chart four times, then work Row 1. The piece should measure approx 18" from beg.

BO in patt.

Front
Work same as Back.

Finishing
Block pieces (see "Blocking" on page 28) to measurements.

Sew three side seams.

Insert pillow form.

Sew remaining side seam.

Twisted Cord
Cut twenty 220" strands of yarn.

Gather strands into a single bunch. With someone holding one end of bunch (or with one end attached to a doorknob), twist strands clockwise until yarn is taut and begins to twist back on itself.

Fold in half to form cord and secure cut ends to prevent unraveling.

Sew cord around edges of pillow to cover side seams, adjusting length if necessary.

PATTERN STITCH KEY

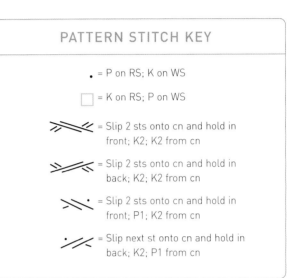

• = P on RS; K on WS

☐ = K on RS; P on WS

= Slip 2 sts onto cn and hold in front; K2; K2 from cn

= Slip 2 sts onto cn and hold in back; K2; K2 from cn

= Slip 2 sts onto cn and hold in front; P1; K2 from cn

= Slip next st onto cn and hold in back; K2; P1 from cn

ENTWINED CABLES PATTERN

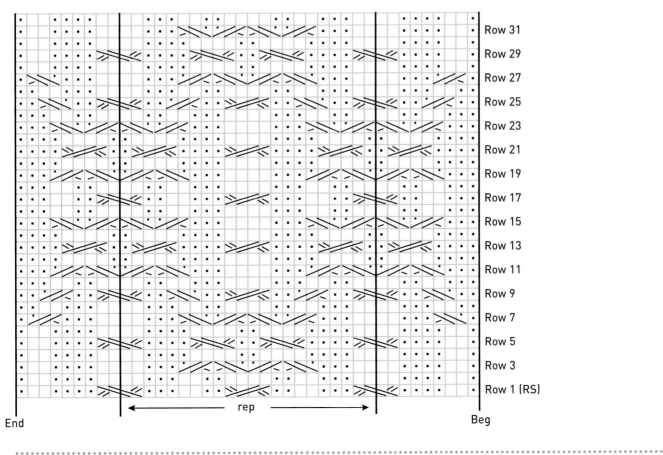

Row 31
Row 29
Row 27
Row 25
Row 23
Row 21
Row 19
Row 17
Row 15
Row 13
Row 11
Row 9
Row 7
Row 5
Row 3
Row 1 (RS)

← rep →

End   Beg

Aran-Style Afghan

A mix of diamonds, bobbles, and Double Seed Stitch grace this throw.
Knotted fringe makes it extra special.

Skill Level
Intermediate

Size
One size

Finished Measurements
Approx 52 x 68" excluding fringe

Materials
- Norwegian Spirit/SandnesGarn's Alfa (5-bulky weight; 85% superwash wool/15% mohair; each approx 1¾ oz/50 g and 65 yd/60 m), 37 balls in #1012 Natural
- One size 10 (6 mm) circular knitting needle, 36" or longer, or size needed to obtain gauge
- One cable needle
- Three stitch markers
- One large crochet hook (for attaching fringe)

Gauge
In Traditional Cable Patt, 18 sts and 22 rows = 4".
To save time, take time to check gauge.

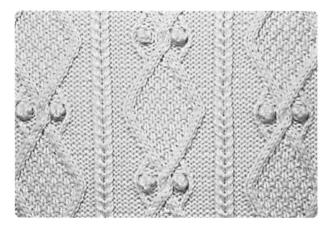

Stitch Patterns
Right Side Double Seed Stitch Pattern *(11-st panel)*
See chart on page 49.

Right Side Cable Pattern *(26-st panel)*
See chart on page 49.

Traditional Cable Pattern *(mult 48 sts)*
See chart on page 49.

Left Side Cable and Double Seed Stitch Pattern *(13-st panel)*
See chart on page 49.

NOTE
- A circular knitting needle is used in order to accommodate the large number of sts; do not join at end of rows.

AFGHAN
CO 242 sts.

Work Row 1 of Right Side Double Seed Stitch Patt across first 11 sts, place marker, work Row 1 of Right Side Cable Patt across next 26 sts, place marker, work Row 1 of Traditional Cable Patt across middle 192 sts, place marker, work Row 1 of Left Side Cable and Double Seed Stitch Patt across next 13 sts to end row.

Cont even in patts as established until piece measures approx 70" from beg, ending after Row 27 of Traditional Cable Patt.

Next Row BO *loosely* in patt on Row 28.

Finishing
Block (see "Blocking" on page 28) to measurements.

Knotted Fringe
For each tuft of fringe, cut three 12" lengths of yarn.

Attach fringe to two short sides of afghan, using knotted fringe technique explained on page 27.

Trim fringe evenly.

PATTERN STITCH KEY

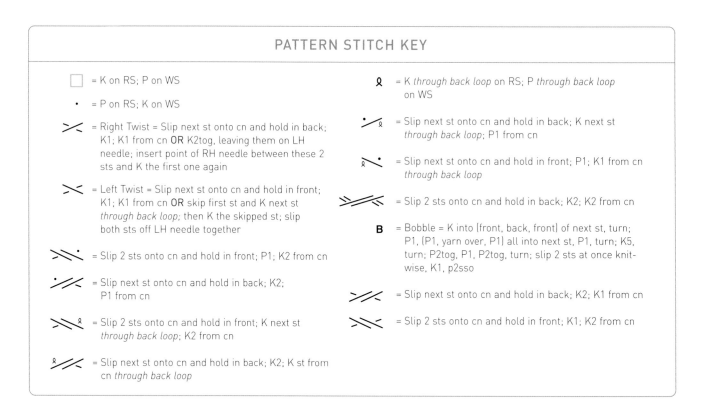

☐ = K on RS; P on WS

• = P on RS; K on WS

⤬ = Right Twist = Slip next st onto cn and hold in back; K1; K1 from cn **OR** K2tog, leaving them on LH needle; insert point of RH needle between these 2 sts and K the first one again

⤬ = Left Twist = Slip next st onto cn and hold in front; K1; K1 from cn **OR** skip first st and K next st *through back loop*; then K the skipped st; slip both sts off LH needle together

⤬• = Slip 2 sts onto cn and hold in front; P1; K2 from cn

•⤬ = Slip next st onto cn and hold in back; K2; P1 from cn

⤬ᶛ = Slip 2 sts onto cn and hold in front; K next st *through back loop*; K2 from cn

ᶛ⤬ = Slip next st onto cn and hold in back; K2; K st from cn *through back loop*

ᶛ = K *through back loop* on RS; P *through back loop* on WS

•ᶛ = Slip next st onto cn and hold in back; K next st *through back loop*; P1 from cn

ᶛ• = Slip next st onto cn and hold in front; P1; K1 from cn *through back loop*

⤬ = Slip 2 sts onto cn and hold in back; K2; K2 from cn

B = Bobble = K into (front, back, front) of next st, turn; P1, (P1, yarn over, P1) all into next st, P1, turn; K5, turn; P2tog, P1, P2tog, turn; slip 2 sts at once knitwise, K1, p2sso

⤬ = Slip next st onto cn and hold in back; K2; K1 from cn

⤬ = Slip 2 sts onto cn and hold in front; K1; K2 from cn

RIGHT SIDE CABLE PATTERN

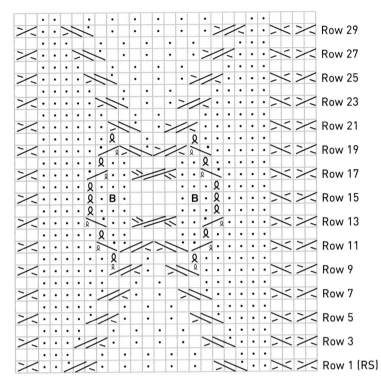

Row 29
Row 27
Row 25
Row 23
Row 21
Row 19
Row 17
Row 15
Row 13
Row 11
Row 9
Row 7
Row 5
Row 3
Row 1 (RS)

RIGHT SIDE DOUBLE SEED STITCH PATTERN

Row 3
Row 1 (RS)

LEFT SIDE CABLE AND DOUBLE SEED STITCH PATTERN

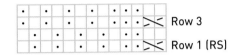

Row 3
Row 1 (RS)

ARAN-STYLE CABLE PATTERN

Row 29
Row 27
Row 25
Row 23
Row 21
Row 19
Row 17
Row 15
Row 13
Row 11
Row 9
Row 7
Row 5
Row 3
Row 1 (RS)

← rep →

Harvest Tweed Afghan

Two strands of yarn held together make this piece extra warm and very quick to make!
It features Axis Cables flanked by simple eyelet lace.

Skill Level
Intermediate

Size
One size

Finished Measurements
Approx 48 x 68" excluding fringe

Materials
- Classic Elite Yarn's Gatsby (5-bulky weight; 70% wool/15% viscose/15% nylon; each approx 3½ oz/100 g and 94 yd/86 m), 14 balls in #2185 Orange Tweed (A)
- Classic Elite Yarn's La Gran (4-worsted weight; 76½% mohair/17½% wool/6% nylon; each approx 1½ oz/42 g and 90 yd/82 m), 15 balls in #6585 Pumpkin (B)
- One size 17 (12.75 mm) circular knitting needle, 29" or longer, or size needed to obtain gauge
- Two cable needles
- One large crochet hook (for attaching fringe)

Gauge
In Seed St Patt with one strand *each* of A and B held tog, 8 sts and 12 rows = 4".
To save time, take time to check gauge.

Stitch Patterns
Seed Stitch Pattern *(mult 2 + 1 sts)*
Row 1 (RS): *K1, P1. Repeat from * across, ending row with K1.
Row 2: As Row 1.
Repeat Rows 1 and 2 for patt.

Cable and Lace Pattern *(mult 17 + 22 sts)*
See chart on page 51.

NOTE
- A circular knitting needle is used in order to accommodate the large number of sts; do not join at end of rows.

AFGHAN
CO 107 sts.

Beg Cable and Lace Patt, and work even until piece measures approx 68" from beg, ending after Row 9 of patt.

Next Row: BO *loosely* in patt on Row 10.

Finishing
Block (see "Blocking" on page 28) to measurements.

Fringe
For each tuft of fringe, using one strand *each* of A and B, cut six 15" lengths of yarn.

Attach fringe to two short sides of afghan. (See "Basic Fringe" on page 27.)

Trim fringe evenly.

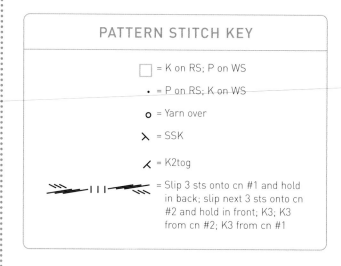

PATTERN STITCH KEY

☐ = K on RS; P on WS

• = P on RS; K on WS

o = Yarn over

⋋ = SSK

⋌ = K2tog

= Slip 3 sts onto cn #1 and hold in back; slip next 3 sts onto cn #2 and hold in front; K3; K3 from cn #2; K3 from cn #1

CABLE AND LACE PATTERN

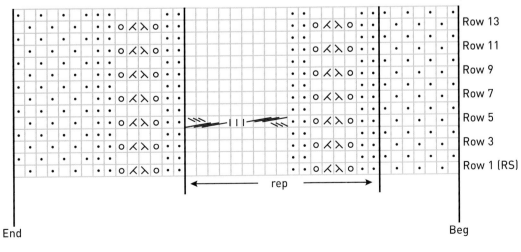

Row 13

Row 11

Row 9

Row 7

Row 5

Row 3

Row 1 (RS)

rep

End

Beg

Rug with Faux Tassels

Traveling Knit Stitches worked in the shape of tassels
create the clever trompe l'oeil border for this throw rug.

Skill Level
Intermediate

Size
One size

Finished Measurements
Approx 30 x 45"

Materials
- Plymouth Yarn Company's Encore Chunky (5-bulky weight; 75% acrylic/25% wool; each approx 3½ oz/50 g and 143 yd/131 m), 8 balls in #180 Rose
- One size 10 (6 mm) circular knitting needle, 24" or longer, or size needed to obtain gauge
- One cable needle

Gauge
In Main Cable Patt, 20 sts and 24 rows = 4"
To save time, take time to check gauge.

Stitch Patterns
Lower Tassel Border Pattern *(mult 16 + 44 sts)*
See chart on page 55.

Main Cable Pattern *(mult 16 + 44 sts)*
See chart on page 54.

Upper Tassel Border Pattern *(mult 16 + 44 sts)*
See chart on page 55.

NOTES
- A circular knitting needle is used in order to accommodate the large number of sts; do not join at end of rows.
- Use your gauge swatch to practice the unusual wrapping technique used in Row 15 of the Main Cable Patt chart. Don't wrap too tightly or you'll create holes in your fabric!

RUG
CO 124 sts.

Beg Lower Tassel Border Patt, and work Rows 1-22.

Beg Main Cable Patt with Row 1. Work even until piece measures approx 41" from beg, ending after Row 16 of patt.

Beg Upper Tassel Border Patt with Row 1, and work Rows 1-20.

BO in patt.

Block (see "Blocking" on page 28) to measurements.

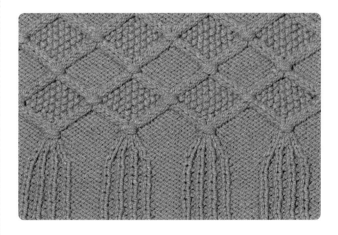

LOWER TASSEL BORDER PATTERN

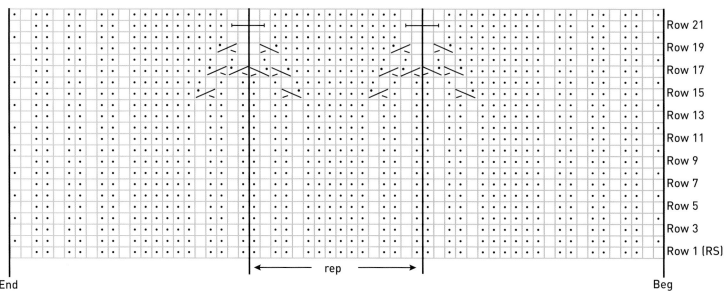

Row 21
Row 19
Row 17
Row 15
Row 13
Row 11
Row 9
Row 7
Row 5
Row 3
Row 1 (RS)

End   ← rep →   Beg

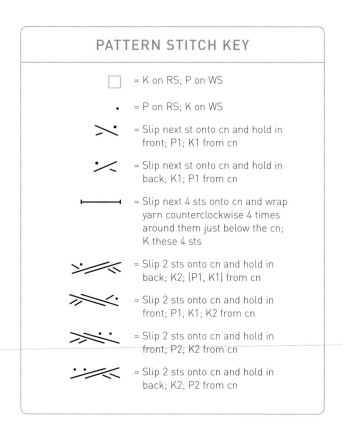

PATTERN STITCH KEY

□ = K on RS; P on WS

• = P on RS; K on WS

= Slip next st onto cn and hold in front; P1; K1 from cn

= Slip next st onto cn and hold in back; K1; P1 from cn

= Slip next 4 sts onto cn and wrap yarn counterclockwise 4 times around them just below the cn; K these 4 sts

= Slip 2 sts onto cn and hold in back; K2; (P1, K1) from cn

= Slip 2 sts onto cn and hold in front; P1, K1; K2 from cn

= Slip 2 sts onto cn and hold in front; P2; K2 from cn

= Slip 2 sts onto cn and hold in back; K2; P2 from cn

MAIN CABLE PATTERN

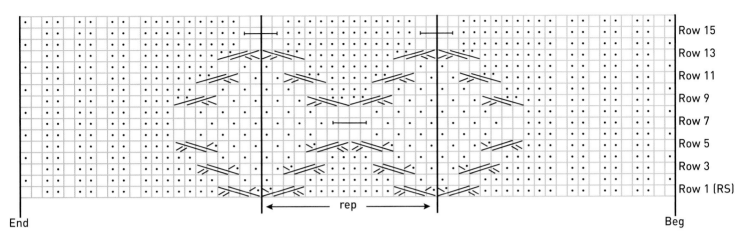

Row 15
Row 13
Row 11
Row 9
Row 7
Row 5
Row 3
Row 1 (RS)

End

← rep →

Beg

UPPER TASSEL BORDER PATTERN

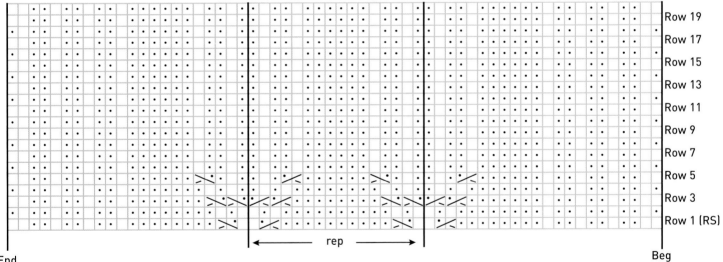

Row 19
Row 17
Row 15
Row 13
Row 11
Row 9
Row 7
Row 5
Row 3
Row 1 (RS)

End

← rep →

Beg

Two-Color Pillow

This project looks more complicated than it actually is to knit. It's just narrow vertical stripes that are cabled every eighth row! A button band on the back makes laundering easy.

Skill Level
Intermediate

Size
One size

Finished Measurements
Approx 18 x 18"

Materials
- Plymouth Yarn Company's Galway (4-worsted weight; 100% wool; each approx 3½ oz/100 g and 210 yd/192 m), 3 balls in #59 Loden (A)
- Three balls of Galway #106 Sage (B)
- One pair of size 8 (5 mm) knitting needles or size needed to obtain gauge
- One cable needle
- One blunt-end yarn needle
- One 18" pillow form
- Five 1" buttons (JHB International's Sonnet, Style #10250 was used on sample pillow)

Gauge
In Two-Color Cable Patt, 28 sts and 24 rows = 4".
To save time, take time to check gauge.

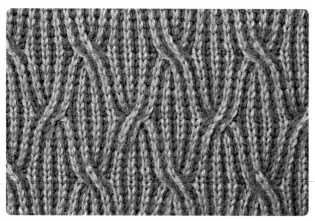

Stitch Patterns
Two-Color Cable Pattern *(mult 14 + 10 sts)*
See chart on page 57.

Garter St Pattern (any number of sts)
Patt Row: Knit across.
Repeat Patt Row for patt.

NOTE
- **When knitting from the chart,** use fair-isle technique, being careful to carry the yarn *loosely* on WS of fabric.

Back
With A, CO 136 sts.

Beg Two-Color Cable Patt. Work even in patt as established until piece measures approx 18" from beg, ending after Row 2 of patt. Break off B. Work only with A to end.

Button Facing
Next Row (RS): Knit, dec 50 sts evenly across—86 sts rem. Cont even in Garter St Patt until button facing measures approx 3" from beg.

BO knitwise.

Front
Work same as Back until piece measures approx 16¼" from beg, ending after Row 2 of patt. Break off B. Work only with A to end.

Next Row (RS): Knit, dec 50 sts evenly across—86 sts rem.

Cont even in Garter St Patt until piece measures approx 17¾" from beg, ending after WS row.

Next Row (Buttonhole Row) (RS): K7, *BO 4 sts, K13. Repeat from * across, ending row with BO 4 sts, K7.

Next Row: Knit across, CO 4 sts over the bound-off sts of previous row.

Cont even in Garter St Patt until piece measures approx 19¼" from beg.

BO knitwise.

Finishing
Block pieces (see "Blocking" on page 28) to measurements.

Sew three side seams, leaving button side open and folding button facing to inside. Sew on buttons to correspond to buttonholes.

Insert pillow form.

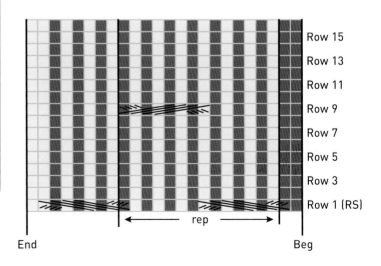

PATTERN STITCH KEY

☐ = K on RS; P on WS

 = Slip 4 sts onto cn and hold in front; K4; K4 from cn

= Slip 4 sts onto cn and hold in back; K4; K4 from cn

Note: Work dark-colored squares with Color A; work light-colored squares with Color B.

TWO-COLOR CABLE PATTERN

Row 15
Row 13
Row 11
Row 9
Row 7
Row 5
Row 3
Row 1 (RS)

← rep →

End   Beg

57

Sampler Afghan

Practice—and showcase—your cabling skills as you create this family heirloom.

Skill Level
Intermediate

Size
One size

Finished Measurements
Approx 52 x 68"

Materials
- Classic Elite Yarns's Montera (4-heavy worsted weight; 50% llama/50% wool; each approx 3½ oz/100 g and 127 yd/116 m), 26 hanks in #3829 Aqua Ice
- One pair of size 9 (5.5 mm) knitting needles or size needed to obtain gauge
- Two cable needles
- One blunt-end yarn needle

Gauge
In Reverse Stockinette St Patt, 16 sts and 24 rows = 4".
To save time, take time to check gauge.

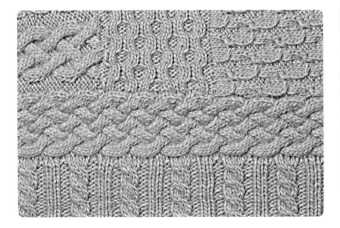

Stitch Patterns
Reverse Stockinette St Pattern *(any number of sts)*
Row 1 (RS): Purl across.
Row 2: Knit across.
Repeat Rows 1 and 2 for patt.

Panel A *(26-st panel)*
See chart on page 62.

Panel B *(38-st motif, inc to 62 sts)*
See chart on page 62.

Panel C *(mult 8 + 2 sts)*
See chart on page 63.

Panel D *(28-st panel)*
See chart on page 63.

Panel E *(mult 12 + 8 sts)*
See chart on page 63.

Panel F *(39-st motif, inc to 57 sts)*
See chart on page 64.

Panel G *(22-st panel)*
See chart on page 64.

NOTES
- **To M1 knitwise slanting to the left:** On RS rows, insert LH needle under the horizontal strand between two sts *from front to back*, and K it *through back loop*.
- **To M1 knitwise slanting to the right:** On RS rows, insert LH needle under the horizontal strand between two sts *from back to front*, and K it *through front loop*.
- **To M1 purlwise slanting to the left:** On RS rows, insert LH needle under the horizontal strand between two sts *from front to back*, and P it *through back loop*.
- **To M1 purlwise slanting to the right:** On RS rows, insert LH needle under the horizontal strand between two sts *from back to front*, and P it *through front loop*.

Panel A
(Make four. Finished measurements: 3¾ x 29")
CO 26 sts.

Beg Panel A chart.

Repeat Rows 1-8 until piece measures approx 29" from beg.

BO in patt.

Panel B
(Make four. Finished measurements: 10 x 15")
CO 38 sts.

Beg Reverse Stockinette St Patt, and work even until piece measures approx 2" from beg, ending after WS row.

Beg Panel B chart, and work Rows 1-30, then work Rows 7-44.

Beg with RS row, work Reverse Stockinette St Patt until piece measures approx 15" from beg.

BO.

Panel C
(Make four. Finished measurements: 6¼ x 15")
CO 34 sts.

Beg Panel C chart.

Repeat Rows 1-12 until piece measures approx 15" from beg.

BO in patt.

Panel D
(Make four. Finished measurements: 4 x 16¼")
CO 28 sts.

Beg Panel D chart.

Repeat Rows 1-8 until piece measures approx 16¼" from beg.

BO in patt.

Panel E
(Make four. Finished measurements: 7¼ x 10")
CO 44 sts.

Beg Panel E chart.

Repeat Rows 1-6 until piece measures approx 10" from beg.

BO in patt.

Panel F
(Make four. Finished measurements: 9 x 10")
CO 39 sts.
Beg Reverse Stockinette St Patt, and work even until piece measures approx 2" from beg, ending after WS row.

Beg Panel F chart, and work Rows 1-36.

Beg with RS row, work Reverse Stockinette St Patt until piece measures approx 10" from beg.

BO.

PANEL B

PANEL F

Panel G
(Make two. Finished measurements: 2¼ x 58")
CO 22 sts.

Beg Panel G chart.

Repeat Rows 1-8 until piece measures approx 58" from beg.

BO in patt.

Finishing
Block Panels (see "Blocking" on page 28) to measurements.

Follow Assembly Illustration at bottom left, with RS facing, sew one each of Panels A, B, C, D, E, and F tog into four matching rectangles, easing fullness of cables. Sew rectangles tog. Sew Panel G to each side of afghan.

Border
With RS facing, pick up and knit 252 sts along one long side of afghan.

Row 1 (WS): P2, *K2, P4, K2, P2. Repeat from * across.

Row 2: K2, M1 knitwise slanting to the right, *P2, K4, P2, K2. Repeat from * across, ending row with P2, K4, P2, M1 knitwise slanting to the left, K2.

Row 3: P3, *K2, P4, K2, P2. Repeat from * across, ending row with K2, P4, K2, P3.

Row 4: K2, M1 knitwise slanting to the right, K1, *P2, slip next 2 sts onto cn and hold in front, K2, K2 from cn, P2, K2. Repeat from * across, ending row with P2, slip next 2 sts onto cn and hold in front, K2, K2 from cn, P2, K1, M1 knitwise slanting to the left, K2.

Row 5: P4, *K2, P4, K2, P2. Repeat from * across, ending row with K2, P4, K2, P4.

Row 6: K2, M1 purlwise slanting to the right, K2, *P2, K4, P2, K2. Repeat from * across, ending row with P2, K4, P2, K2, M1 purlwise slanting to the left, K2.

Row 7: P2, K1, P2, *K2, P4, K2, P2. Repeat from * across, ending row with K1, P2.

Row 8: K2, M1 purlwise slanting to the right, P1, *K2, P2, slip next 2 sts onto cn and hold in front, K2, K2 from cn, P2. Repeat from * across, ending row with K2, P2, slip next 2 sts onto cn and hold in front, K2, K2 from cn, P2, K2, P1, M1 purlwise slanting to the left, K2.

Row 9: P2, K2, *P2, K2, P4, K2. Repeat from * across, ending row with P2, K2, P2.

Row 10: K2, M1 knitwise slanting to the right, *P2, K2, P2, K4. Repeat from * across, ending row with P2, K2, P2, M1 knitwise slanting to the left, K2.

Row 11: P3, *K2, P2, K2, P4. Repeat from * across, ending row with K2, P2, K2, P3.

Row 12: K2, M1 knitwise slanting to the right, K1, *P2, K2, P2, slip next 2 sts onto cn and hold in front, K2, K2 from cn. Repeat from * across, ending row with P2, K2, P2, K1, M1 knitwise slanting to the left, K2.

Row 13: P4, *K2, P2, K2, P4. Repeat from * across.

Row 14: K2, M1 knitwise slanting to the right, K2, *P2, K2, P2, K4. Repeat from * across, ending row with P2, K2, P2, K2, M1 knitwise slanting to the left, K2.

Row 15: P5, *K2, P2, K2, P4. Repeat from * across, ending row with P1.

Row 16: K2, M1 knitwise slanting to the right, K3, *P2, K2, P2, slip next 2 sts onto cn and hold in front, K2, K2 from cn. Repeat from * across, ending row with P2, K2, P2, K3, M1 knitwise slanting to the left, K2.

Row 17: P6, *K2, P2, K2, P4. Repeat from * across, ending row with P2.

Row 18: K2, M1 purlwise slanting to the right, K4, *P2, K2, P2, K4. Repeat from * across, ending row with M1 purlwise slanting to the left, K2.

Row 19: P2, K1, P4, *K2, P2, K2, P4. Repeat from * across, ending row with K1, P2.

Row 20: K2, M1 purlwise slanting to the right, P1, *slip next 2 sts onto cn and hold in front, K2, K2 from cn, P2, K2, P2. Repeat from * across, ending row with slip next 2 sts onto cn and hold in front, K2, K2 from cn, P1, M1 purlwise slanting to the left, K2.

Row 21: P2, K2, *P4, K2, P2, K2. Repeat from * across, ending row with P4, K2, P2.

BO *loosely* in patt.

Repeat for other long side.

With RS facing, pick up and knit 212 sts along one short side of afghan. Work same as first side of edging.

BO *loosely* in patt.

Repeat for other short side.

Using Mattress St (see "Mattress Stitch Seam" on page 28), sew corners tog.

PANEL A

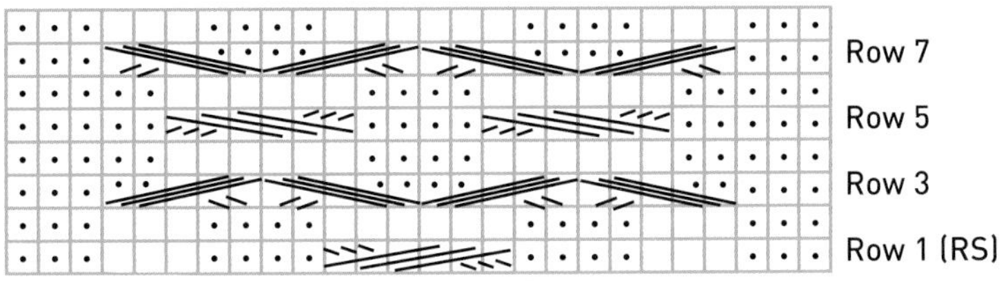

Row 7
Row 5
Row 3
Row 1 (RS)

PANEL B

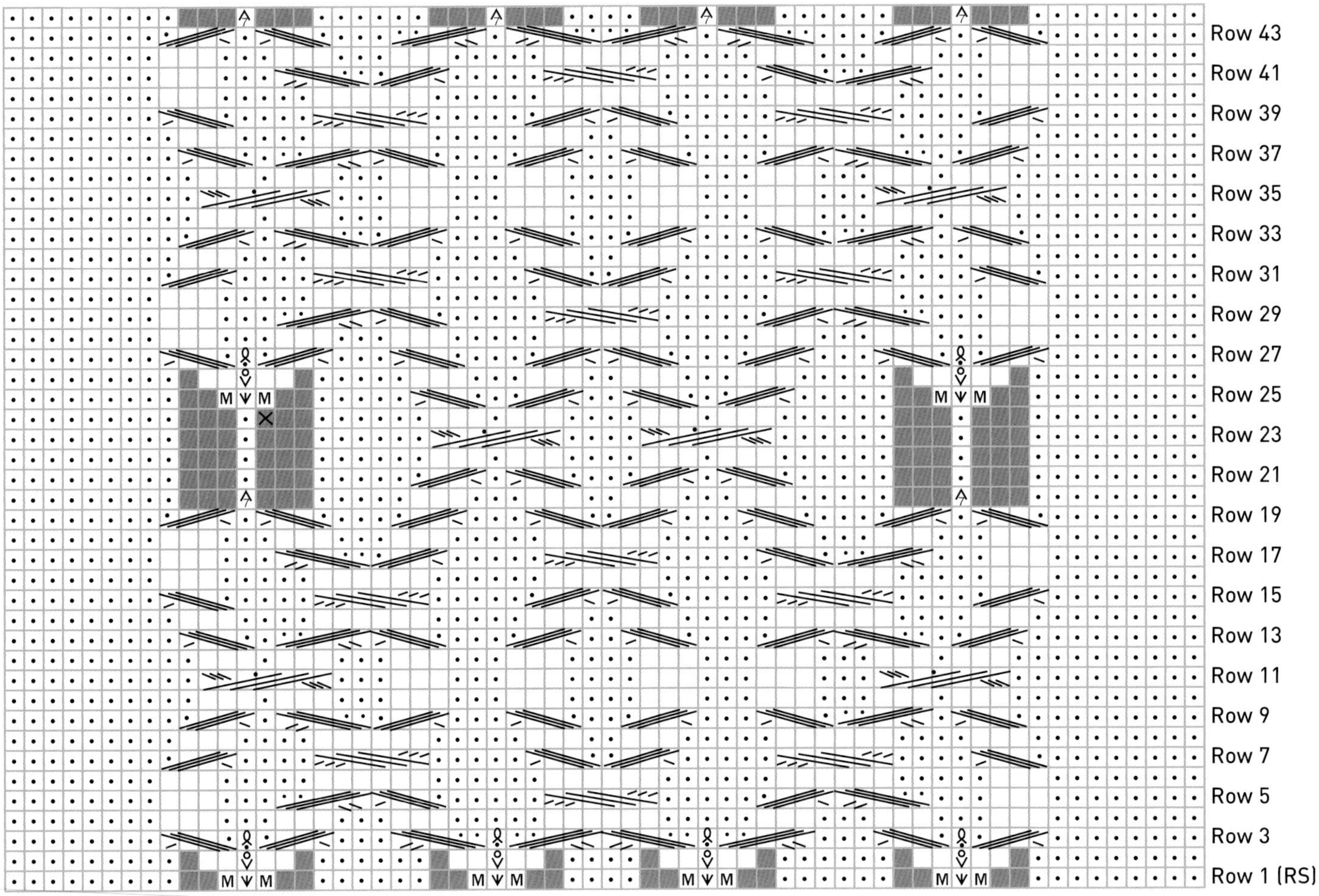

Row 43
Row 41
Row 39
Row 37
Row 35
Row 33
Row 31
Row 29
Row 27
Row 25
Row 23
Row 21
Row 19
Row 17
Row 15
Row 13
Row 11
Row 9
Row 7
Row 5
Row 3
Row 1 (RS)

PATTERN STITCH KEY

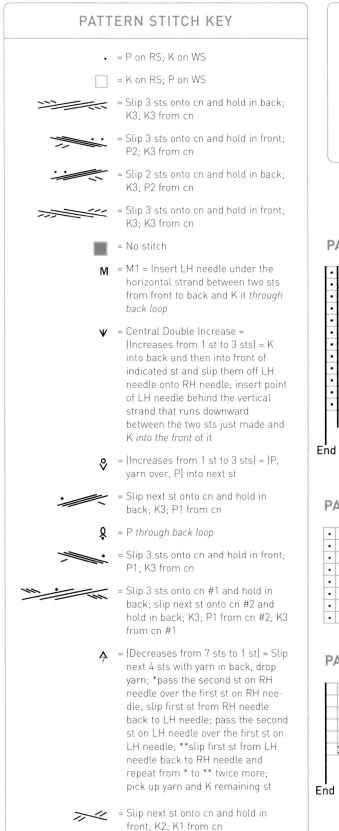

• = P on RS; K on WS

□ = K on RS; P on WS

= Slip 3 sts onto cn and hold in back; K3; K3 from cn

= Slip 3 sts onto cn and hold in front; P2; K3 from cn

= Slip 2 sts onto cn and hold in back; K3; P2 from cn

= Slip 3 sts onto cn and hold in front; K3; K3 from cn

= No stitch

M = M1 = Insert LH needle under the horizontal strand between two sts from front to back and K it *through back loop*

⋎ = Central Double Increase = (Increases from 1 st to 3 sts) = K into back and then into front of indicated st and slip them off LH needle onto RH needle; insert point of LH needle behind the vertical strand that runs downward between the two sts just made and K *into the front* of it

⏦ = (Increases from 1 st to 3 sts) = (P, yarn over, P) into next st

= Slip next st onto cn and hold in back; K3; P1 from cn

⍨ = P *through back loop*

= Slip 3 sts onto cn and hold in front; P1; K3 from cn

= Slip 3 sts onto cn #1 and hold in back; slip next st onto cn #2 and hold in back; K3; P1 from cn #2; K3 from cn #1

⋀ = (Decreases from 7 sts to 1 st) = Slip next 4 sts with yarn in back, drop yarn; *pass the second st on RH needle over the first st on RH needle; slip first st from RH needle back to LH needle; pass the second st on LH needle over the first st on LH needle; **slip first st from LH needle back to RH needle and repeat from * to ** twice more; pick up yarn and K remaining st

= Slip next st onto cn and hold in front; K2; K1 from cn

= Slip 2 sts onto cn and hold in back; K1; K2 from cn

= Slip 2 sts onto cn and hold in front; P2; K2 from cn

= Slip 2 sts onto cn and hold in back; K2; K2 from cn

= Slip 2 sts onto cn and hold in back; K2; P2 from cn

PANEL C

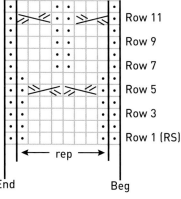

Row 11
Row 9
Row 7
Row 5
Row 3
Row 1 (RS)

←— rep —→

End   Beg

PANEL D

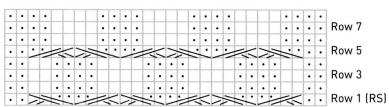

Row 7
Row 5
Row 3
Row 1 (RS)

PANEL E

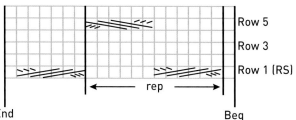

Row 5
Row 3
Row 1 (RS)

←—— rep ——→

End   Beg

PANEL F

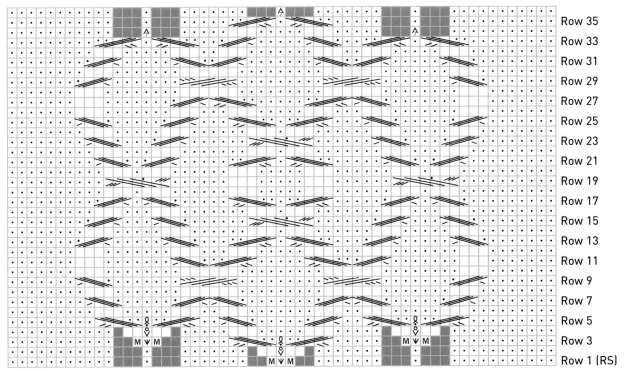

Row 35
Row 33
Row 31
Row 29
Row 27
Row 25
Row 23
Row 21
Row 19
Row 17
Row 15
Row 13
Row 11
Row 9
Row 7
Row 5
Row 3
Row 1 (RS)

PANEL G

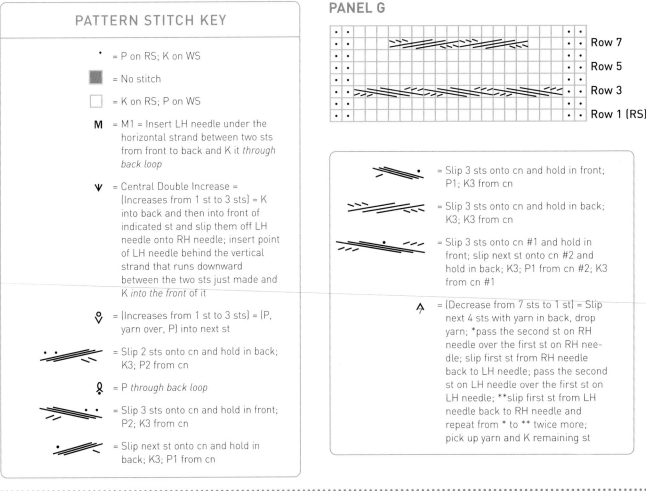

Row 7
Row 5
Row 3
Row 1 (RS)

PATTERN STITCH KEY

• = P on RS; K on WS

■ = No stitch

□ = K on RS; P on WS

M = M1 = Insert LH needle under the horizontal strand between two sts from front to back and K it *through back loop*

Ⓥ = Central Double Increase = (Increases from 1 st to 3 sts) = K into back and then into front of indicated st and slip them off LH needle onto RH needle; insert point of LH needle behind the vertical strand that runs downward between the two sts just made and K *into the front* of it

⌄ = (Increases from 1 st to 3 sts) = (P, yarn over, P) into next st

= Slip 2 sts onto cn and hold in back; K3; P2 from cn

Ⓧ = P *through back loop*

= Slip 3 sts onto cn and hold in front; P2; K3 from cn

= Slip next st onto cn and hold in back; K3; P1 from cn

= Slip 3 sts onto cn and hold in front; P1; K3 from cn

= Slip 3 sts onto cn and hold in back; K3; K3 from cn

= Slip 3 sts onto cn #1 and hold in front; slip next st onto cn #2 and hold in back; K3; P1 from cn #2; K3 from cn #1

⋏ = (Decrease from 7 sts to 1 st) = Slip next 4 sts with yarn in back, drop yarn; *pass the second st on RH needle over the first st on RH needle; slip first st from RH needle back to LH needle; pass the second st on LH needle over the first st on LH needle; **slip first st from LH needle back to RH needle and repeat from * to ** twice more; pick up yarn and K remaining st

Chapter 4

Cable Chic

·······················

CLOTHING
FOR WOMEN

Intricate or simple, sporty or elegant, cable-knit sweaters are staples in our daily wardrobes. With seemingly endless design variations, they can be classic fisherman-style pullovers or sexy, chic garments from today's (and tomorrow's!) top couture designers.

The collection in this book offers a bit of both, from a classic cable and ribbed raglan design and traditional tweedy saddle-shoulder pullover to a hip poncho and sassy skirt with fringe. You'll enjoy knitting—and wearing—these pieces. Their timeless style will always be in fashion.

Tweed Pullover

You'll enjoy creating and showing off this richly cabled sweater.
The vertical panels on the sleeves and saddle-shoulders make it particularly flattering!

Skill Level
Experienced

Sizes
Small (Medium, Large, 1X, 2X). Instructions are for smallest size, with changes for other sizes noted in parentheses as necessary.

Finished Measurements
Bust: 37½ (41, 44, 47½, 50½)"
Total length: 26¾"

Materials
- Westminster Fibers/Rowan's Scottish Tweed DK (3-DK weight; 100% wool; each approx 1¾ oz/50 g and 123 yd/113 m), 14 (16, 18, 20, 22) balls in #003 Skye
- One pair *each* of sizes 5 and 6 (3.75 and 4 mm) knitting needles or size needed to obtain gauge
- Two cable needles
- Two stitch markers
- One blunt-end yarn needle

Gauge
In Diamond Cable Patt with larger needles, 27 sts and 28 rows = 4".
To save time, take time to check gauge.

Stitch Patterns
Diamond Cable Pattern (mult 22 sts)
See chart on page 71.

Sleeve Side Pattern (mult 9 + 5 sts)
See chart on page 72.

Center Sleeve Panel (28-st panel)
See chart on page 72.

Neckband Cable Pattern (mult 9 + 2 sts)
See chart on page 72.

NOTE
- **For sweater assembly,** refer to the illustration for square indented saddle-shoulder construction on page 29.

Back
With smaller needles, CO 128 (140, 150, 162, 172) sts.

Beg Diamond Cable Patt where indicated, and work Rows 1-22.

Change to larger needles, and work Rows 23-48, then repeat Rows 17-48 until piece measures approx 17¼ (17¼, 16¾, 16¼, 15¾)" from beg, ending after WS row.

Shape Armholes
BO 11 (17, 22, 17, 22) sts at beg of next two rows—106 (106, 106, 128, 128) sts rem.

Cont even in patt as established until piece measures approx 23¾" from beg, ending after WS row.

Shape Shoulders
BO 8 (8, 8, 10, 10) sts at beg of next six rows, then BO 6 (6, 6, 11, 11) sts at beg of next two rows—46 sts rem.

BO.

Front
Work same as Back until piece measures approx 23¼" from beg, ending after Row 44 of Diamond Cable Patt.

Shape Neck
Next Row (RS): Work across first 34 (34, 34, 45, 45) sts; join second ball of yarn and BO middle 38 sts, work to end row.

Work both sides at once with separate balls of yarn, and BO 3 sts each neck edge once—31 (31, 31, 42, 42) sts rem each side.

Dec 1 st each neck edge once—30 (30, 30, 41, 41) sts rem each side.

Cont even, if necessary, until piece measures same as Back.

Shape Shoulders
Work same as for Back.

BO.

Sleeves
With larger needles, CO 56 sts.

Set Up Patts
Work Row 1 of Sleeve Side Patt over first 14 sts, place marker, work Row 1 of Center Sleeve Panel, place marker, work Row 1 of Sleeve Side Patt to end row.

Cont patts as established, and inc 1 st each side every fourth row 0 (0, 0, 6, 12) times, every sixth row 7 (6, 18, 18, 14) times, then every eighth row 12 (13, 4, 0, 0) times, working new sts into Sleeve Side Patt on each side—94 (94, 100, 104, 108) sts.

Cont even in patts as established until piece measures approx 20¾ (21, 21, 20, 20)" from beg, ending after WS row.

Shape Saddle
BO 33 (33, 36, 38, 40) sts at beg of next two rows—28 sts rem.

Cont even in patts as established until saddle measures approx 4½ (4½, 4½, 6, 6)" from beg.

BO.

Finishing
Block (see "Blocking" on page 28) to measurements.

Set in Sleeves, leaving left back shoulder seam unsewn.

Neck Edging
With RS facing, pick up and knit 101 sts along neckline.

Beg with Row 2 of Neckband Cable Patt, and work even until band measures approx 4" from beg.

BO in patt.

Sew left shoulder seam.

Sew sleeve and side seams.

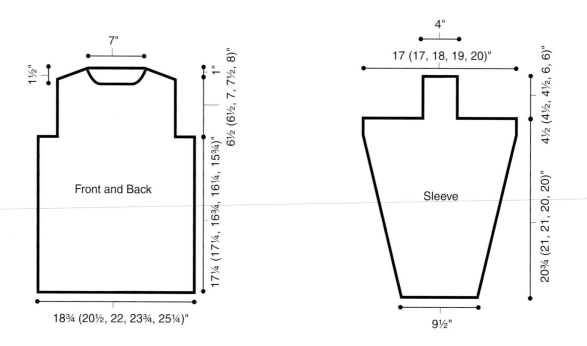

7"
1½"
1"
6½ (6½, 7, 7½, 8)"
Front and Back
17¼ (17¼, 16¾, 16¼, 15¾)"
18¾ (20½, 22, 23¾, 25¼)"

4"
17 (17, 18, 19, 20)"
4½ (4½, 4½, 6, 6)"
Sleeve
20¾ (21, 21, 20, 20)"
9½"

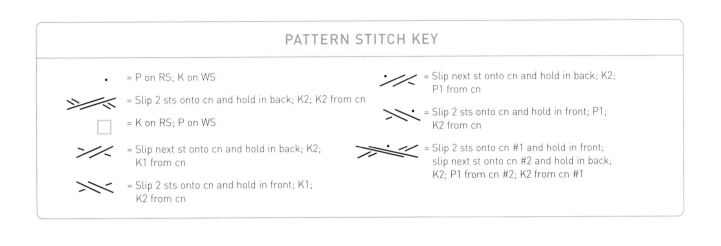

PATTERN STITCH KEY

- • = P on RS; K on WS
- = Slip 2 sts onto cn and hold in back; K2; K2 from cn
- □ = K on RS; P on WS
- = Slip next st onto cn and hold in back; K2; K1 from cn
- = Slip 2 sts onto cn and hold in front; K1; K2 from cn
- = Slip next st onto cn and hold in back; K2; P1 from cn
- = Slip 2 sts onto cn and hold in front; P1; K2 from cn
- = Slip 2 sts onto cn #1 and hold in front; slip next st onto cn #2 and hold in back; K2; P1 from cn #2; K2 from cn #1

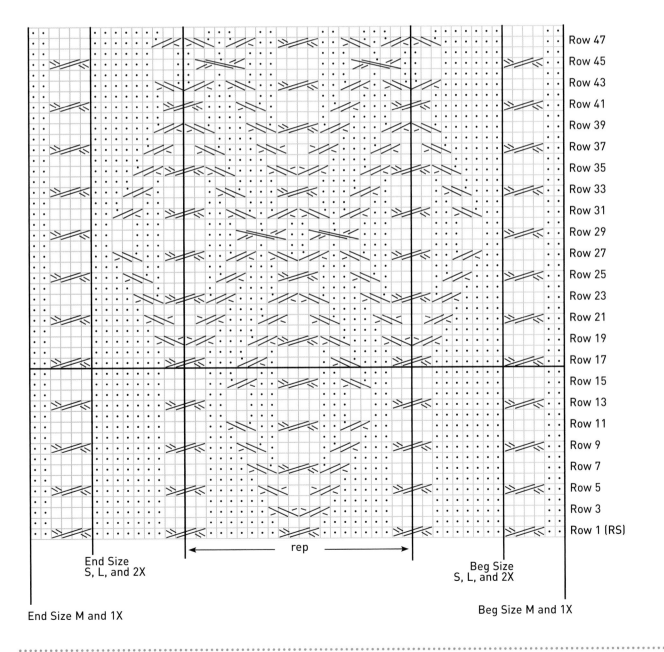

Row 47
Row 45
Row 43
Row 41
Row 39
Row 37
Row 35
Row 33
Row 31
Row 29
Row 27
Row 25
Row 23
Row 21
Row 19
Row 17
Row 15
Row 13
Row 11
Row 9
Row 7
Row 5
Row 3
Row 1 (RS)

rep

End Size
S, L, and 2X

Beg Size
S, L, and 2X

End Size M and 1X

Beg Size M and 1X

PATTERN STITCH KEY

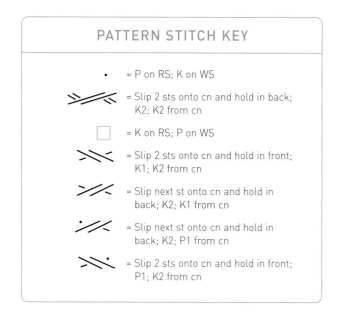

- • = P on RS; K on WS
- = Slip 2 sts onto cn and hold in back; K2; K2 from cn
- ☐ = K on RS; P on WS
- = Slip 2 sts onto cn and hold in front; K1; K2 from cn
- = Slip next st onto cn and hold in back; K2; K1 from cn
- = Slip next st onto cn and hold in back; K2; P1 from cn
- = Slip 2 sts onto cn and hold in front; P1; K2 from cn

SLEEVE SIDE PATTERN

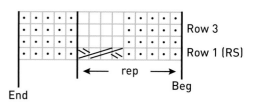

Row 3
Row 1 (RS)
End
rep
Beg

NECKBAND CABLE PATTERN

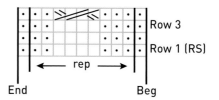

Row 3
Row 1 (RS)
End
rep
Beg

CENTER SLEEVE PANEL

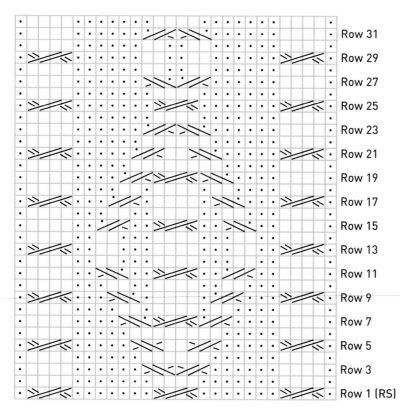

Row 31
Row 29
Row 27
Row 25
Row 23
Row 21
Row 19
Row 17
Row 15
Row 13
Row 11
Row 9
Row 7
Row 5
Row 3
Row 1 (RS)

Poncho

Simple Rope Cables travel up the body of this poncho, culminating in a pretty yoke pattern.
Made in the round from the bottom up, it's a fun project to knit.
Those knitted rounds get shorter and faster as you go!

Skill Level
Intermediate

Size
One size fits most adult women

Finished Measurements
Circumference at top: Approx 23"
Circumference at lower edge: Approx 62"
Total length: 18"

Materials
- Aurora Yarn/Garnstudio's **Eskimo** (6-super bulky weight; 100% wool; each approx 1¾ oz/50 g and 54 yd/50 m), 11 balls in #5 Deep Ocean
- One size 13 (9 mm) circular knitting needle, 36" long, or size needed to obtain gauge
- One size 13 (9 mm) circular knitting needle, 24" long, or size needed to obtain gauge
- One stitch marker
- One cable needle

Gauge
In Cable B Patt, 12 sts and 16 rnds = 4".
To save time, take time to check gauge.

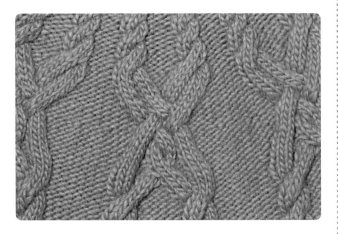

Stitch Patterns
Cable A Pattern *(mult 14 sts)*
See chart on page 76.

Cable B Pattern *(mult 14 sts)*
See chart on page 76.

Cable C Pattern *(mult 28 sts, dec to mult 24 sts)*
See chart on page 76.

Cable D Pattern *(mult 24 sts, dec to mult 20 sts)*
See chart on page 76.

Cable E Pattern *(mult 20 sts, dec to mult 14 sts)*
See chart on page 76.

Cable F Pattern *(mult 14 sts, dec to mult 12 sts)*
See chart on page 76.

Cable G Pattern *(mult 6 sts)*
See chart on page 76.

NOTE
- Change to shorter circular needle when there are no longer enough sts to knit comfortably with the longer circular needle.

PONCHO
With larger circular needle, CO 196 sts. Join, and place marker to indicate beg of rnd.

Work Rnds 1-6 of Cable A Patt.

Beg Cable B Patt, and repeat Rnds 1-6 of chart five times total.

Work Rnds 1-12 of Cable C Patt—168 sts rem.

Work Rnds 1-10 of Cable D Patt—140 sts rem.

Work Rnds 1-4 of Cable E Patt—84 sts rem.

Work Rnds 1-8 of Cable F Patt—72 sts rem.

Work Rnds 1-3 of Cable G Patt, binding off *loosely* in patt on last rnd.

Finishing
Block (see "Blocking" on page 28) to measurements.

CABLE A PATTERN

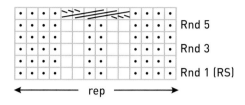

Rnd 5

Rnd 3

Rnd 1 (RS)

rep

CABLE B PATTERN

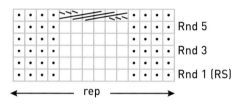

Rnd 5

Rnd 3

Rnd 1 (RS)

rep

CABLE C PATTERN

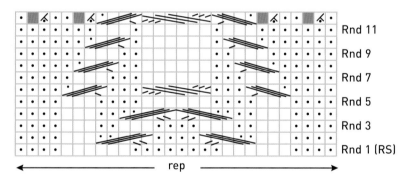

Rnd 11

Rnd 9

Rnd 7

Rnd 5

Rnd 3

Rnd 1 (RS)

rep

CABLE D PATTERN

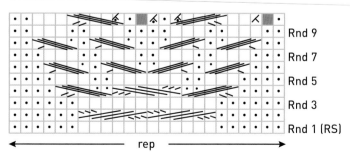

Rnd 9

Rnd 7

Rnd 5

Rnd 3

Rnd 1 (RS)

rep

CABLE E PATTERN

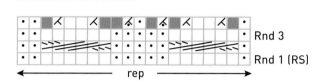

Rnd 3

Rnd 1 (RS)

rep

CABLE F PATTERN

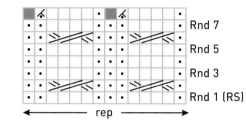

Rnd 7

Rnd 5

Rnd 3

Rnd 1 (RS)

rep

CABLE G PATTERN

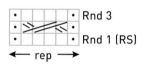

Rnd 3

Rnd 1 (RS)

rep

PATTERN STITCH KEY

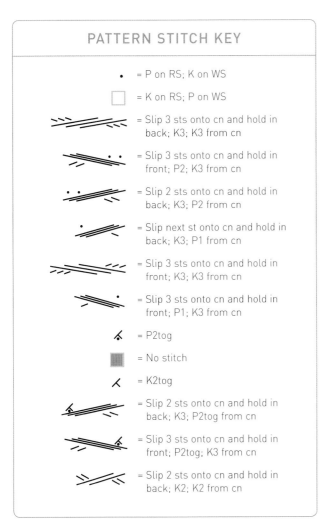

•	= P on RS; K on WS
☐	= K on RS; P on WS
	= Slip 3 sts onto cn and hold in back; K3; K3 from cn
	= Slip 3 sts onto cn and hold in front; P2; K3 from cn
	= Slip 2 sts onto cn and hold in back; K3; P2 from cn
	= Slip next st onto cn and hold in back; K3; P1 from cn
	= Slip 3 sts onto cn and hold in front; K3; K3 from cn
	= Slip 3 sts onto cn and hold in front; P1; K3 from cn
	= P2tog
	= No stitch
	= K2tog
	= Slip 2 sts onto cn and hold in back; K3; P2tog from cn
	= Slip 3 sts onto cn and hold in front; P2tog; K3 from cn
	= Slip 2 sts onto cn and hold in back; K2; K2 from cn

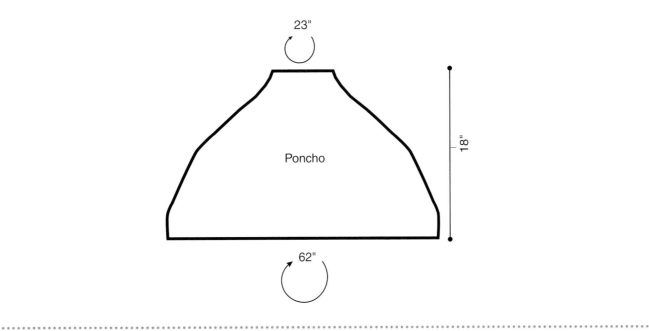

23"

Poncho

18"

62"

Fringed Skirt

Believe it or not, a knitted skirt can be quite flattering to one's figure!
The vertical arrangement of cables makes this one especially slimming.

Skill Level
Intermediate

Sizes
Small (Medium, Large, 1X). Instructions are for smallest size, with changes for other sizes noted in parentheses as necessary.

Finished Measurements
Hip: 31½ (37, 42, 47)"
Total length: 19" excluding fringe

Materials
- Westminster Fibers/Jaeger's Extra Fine Merino DK (3-DK weight; 100% wool; each approx 1¾ oz/50 g and 136 yd/125 m), 8 (9, 10, 11) balls in #973 Biscuit
- One pair *each* of sizes 4 and 5 (3.5 and 3.75 mm) knitting needles or size needed to obtain gauge
- One cable needle
- One blunt-end yarn needle
- elastic, ¾" wide, cut to fit waist

Gauge
In Main Cable Patt with larger needles, 34 sts and 36 rows = 4". **To save time, take time to check gauge.**

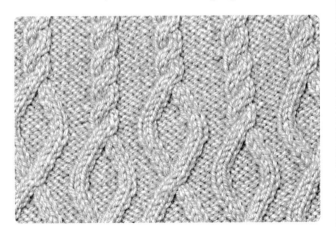

Stitch Patterns
Main Cable Pattern *(mult 22 + 2 sts)*
See chart on page 80.

Yoke Cable Pattern *(mult 22 + 2 sts, dec to 18 + 2 sts)*
See chart on page 80.

Back
With larger needles, CO 134 (156, 178, 200) sts.

Beg Main Cable Patt, and work even until piece measures approx 14" from beg (or 5" short of desired length to waist), ending after Row 16 of patt.

Next Row (RS): Beg Yoke Cable Patt, and follow chart until Row 36 has been completed, working dec as indicated— 110 (128, 146, 164) sts rem.

Waistband
Change to smaller needles, and repeat Rows 33-36 of Yoke Cable Patt six times.

BO *loosely* in patt.

Front
Work same as Back.

Finishing
Block pieces (see "Blocking" on page 28) to measurements.

Sew side seams.

Fold waistband in half to WS, insert elastic, and *loosely* sew into place.

Fringe
For each tuft of fringe, cut six 11" lengths of yarn.

Attach fringe evenly spaced along lower edge of skirt. (See "Basic Fringe" on page 27.)

Trim fringe evenly.

PATTERN STITCH KEY

- • = P on RS; K on WS

- ☐ = K on RS; P on WS

- = Slip 2 sts onto cn and hold in back; K2; K2 from cn

- = Slip 2 sts onto cn and hold in front; P1; K2 from cn

- = Slip next st onto cn and hold in back; K2; P1 from cn

- = P2tog

- ▨ = No stitch

MAIN CABLE PATTERN

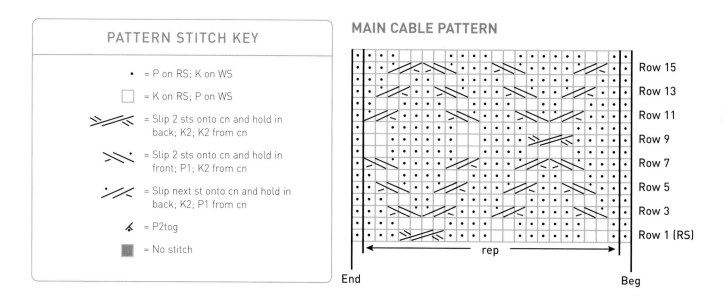

Row 15
Row 13
Row 11
Row 9
Row 7
Row 5
Row 3
Row 1 (RS)

← rep →

End   Beg

13¾ (16, 18¼, 20½)"

1"
1"
4"

Front and Back

14"

15¾ (18½, 21, 23½)"

YOKE CABLE PATTERN

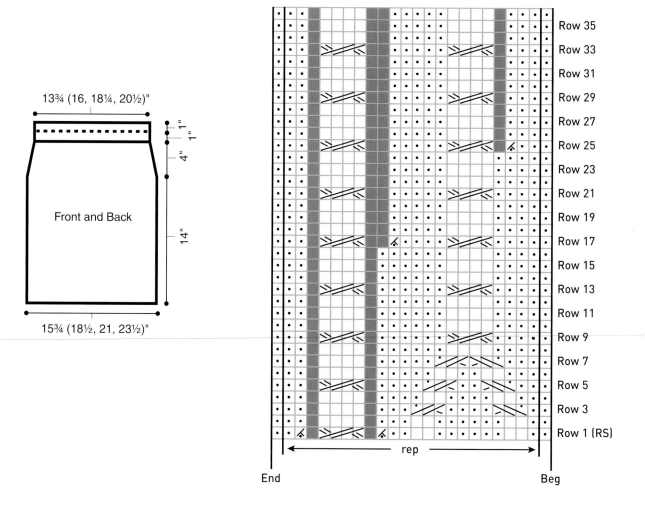

Row 35
Row 33
Row 31
Row 29
Row 27
Row 25
Row 23
Row 21
Row 19
Row 17
Row 15
Row 13
Row 11
Row 9
Row 7
Row 5
Row 3
Row 1 (RS)

← rep →

End   Beg

Cotton Raglan

In this design, the cable pattern appears to continue diagonally along the armhole, drawing the eye upward. It not only flatters the figure, but also points out the pretty neckline!

Skill Level
Intermediate

Sizes
Small (Medium, Large, 1X, 2X). Instructions are for smallest size, with changes for other sizes noted in parentheses as necessary.

Finished Measurements
Bust: 34½ (39½, 44, 49, 54)"
Total length: 22 (22½, 23, 23½, 24)"

Materials
- Skacel Collection/Schulana's Super Cotton (4-worsted weight; 70% cotton/30% polyester; each approx 1¾ oz/ 50 g and 98 yd/90 m), 18 (20, 22, 24, 26) balls in #32 Turquoise
- One pair of size 9 (5.5 mm) knitting needles or size needed to obtain gauge
- One cable needle
- One blunt-end yarn needle

Gauge
In Cable Rib Patt, 26 sts and 28 rows = 4".
To save time, take time to check gauge.

Stitch Pattern
Cable Rib Pattern *(mult 16 + 2 sts)*
See chart at right.

Neckband Pattern *(21-st panel)*
See chart at right.

PATTERN STITCH KEY

☐ = K on RS; P on WS

= Slip 2 sts onto cn and hold in front; K2; K2 from cn

• = P on RS; K on WS

= Right Twist = Slip next st onto cn and hold in back; K1; K1 from cn **OR** K2tog, leaving them on LH needle; insert point of RH needle between these 2 sts and K the first one again

= Left Twist = Slip next st onto cn and hold in front; K1; K1 from cn **OR** skip first st and K next st *in back loop*; then K the skipped st; slip both sts off LH needle together

= Slip 2 sts onto cn and hold in back; K2; K2 from cn

CABLE RIB PATTERN

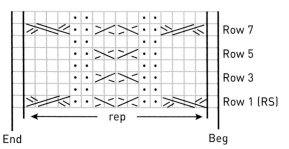

Row 7
Row 5
Row 3
Row 1 (RS)

End ←— rep —→ Beg

NECKBAND PATTERN

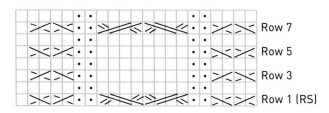

Row 7
Row 5
Row 3
Row 1 (RS)

NOTES

- **For fully-fashioned raglan decreases:** On RS rows, work patt as established across first 6 sts, P2tog, work across in patt as established until 8 sts rem, ending row with SSP, work patt as established to end row; on WS rows, work patt as established across first 6 sts, SSK, work across in patt as established until 8 sts rem in row, ending row with K2tog, work patt as established to end row.
- **For fully-fashioned increases:** On RS rows, work patt as established across first 7 sts, M1, work across in patt as established until 7 sts rem, ending row with M1, work patt as established to end row.
- **For ease in finishing,** instructions include one selvedge st each side; these sts are not reflected in final measurements.
- **For sweater assembly,** refer to the illustration for raglan construction on page 29.

Back
CO 114 (130, 146, 162, 178) sts.

Beg Cable Rib Patt, and work even until piece measures approx 12¾" from beg, ending after WS row.

Shape Raglan
Work fully-fashioned raglan decreases each side on next row and then every other row 20 (16, 11, 7, 2) times, then every row 14 (26, 39, 51, 64) times—44 sts rem.

BO in patt.

Front
Work same as Back until 72 sts rem, ending after WS row.

Shape Neck
Next Row (RS): Work patt as established across first 6 sts, P2tog, work patt as established across next 19 sts; join second ball of yarn and BO middle 18 sts, work patt as established across next 19 sts, SSP, work patt as established to end row—26 sts rem each side.

Work both sides at once with separate balls of yarn, cont raglan shaping same as Back, *and at the same time*, BO 4 sts each neck edge two times, then BO 2 sts each neck edge once, and dec 1 st at neck edge once—8 sts rem each side. Dec 1 st at neck edge every row four times—4 sts rem.

Next Row (RS): (K2tog) two times—2 sts rem.

Next Row: P2tog.

BO.

Sleeves
CO 50 (50, 66, 66, 66) sts.

Beg Cable Rib Patt, and work fully-fashioned increases each side on next row and then every fourth row 14 (14, 0, 12, 12) times, every sixth row 9 (9, 4, 11, 11) times, then every eighth row 0 (0, 11, 0, 0) times—98 (98, 98, 114, 114) sts.

Cont even until piece measures approx 17½ (18, 18, 18, 18)" from beg, ending after WS row.

Shape Raglan
Work fully-fashioned raglan decreases each side on next row and then every other row 15 (19, 22, 18, 21) times, then every row 24 (20, 17, 29, 26) times—18 sts rem.

BO in patt.

Finishing
Block pieces (see "Blocking" on page 28) to measurements.

Sew raglan seams.

Neckband
CO 21 sts.

Work Neckband Patt until piece, when slightly stretched, fits around neckline of sweater.

BO in patt.

Sew Stockinette St selvedge line of neckband into neckline, sewing cast-on and bind-off edges tog at center back of neck.

Sew sleeve and side seams.

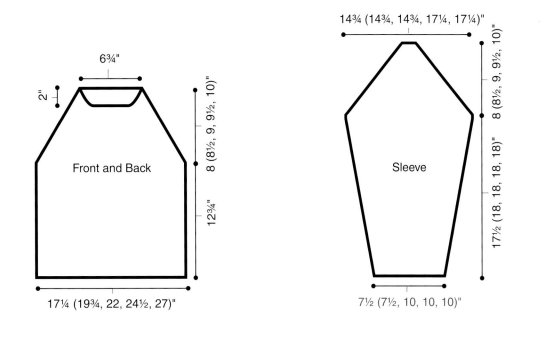

6¾"

2"

Front and Back

8 (8½, 9, 9½, 10)"

12¾"

17¼ (19¾, 22, 24½, 27)"

14¾ (14¾, 14¾, 17¼, 17¼)"

Sleeve

8 (8½, 9, 9½, 10)"

17½ (18, 18, 18, 18)"

7½ (7½, 10, 10, 10)"

Turtleneck

An intricate Allover Cable pattern makes this sweater special.

If you'd prefer a crewneck instead of the turtleneck, bind off your neckband when it's an inch or so high.

Skill Level
Intermediate

Sizes
Small (Medium, Large, 1X). Instructions are for smallest size, with changes for other sizes noted in parentheses as necessary.

Finished Measurements
Bust: 37 (42½, 48, 53½)"
Total length: 21 (21½, 22, 22½)"

Materials
- Tahki-Stacy Charles/Filatura di Crosa's Zara (3-DK weight; 100% wool; each approx 1¾ oz/50 g and 137 yd/125 m), 18 (19, 21, 22) balls in #1718 Cantaloupe
- One pair *each* of sizes 6 and 7 (4 and 4.5 mm) knitting needles or size needed to obtain gauge
- One cable needle
- One blunt-end yarn needle

Gauge
In Main Cable Patt with smaller needles, 35 sts and 28 rows = 4". **To save time, take time to check gauge.**

Stitch Patterns
Cabled Rib Pattern *(mult 12 sts)*
See chart on page 88.

Main Cable Pattern *(mult 24 + 20 sts)*
See chart on page 89.

Stockinette St Pattern *(any number of sts)*
Row 1 (RS): Knit across.
Row 2: Purl across.
Repeat Rows 1 and 2 for patt.

NOTES
- **For fully-fashioned single decreases on front and back of sweater:** On RS rows, K3, SSK, work across in patt as established until 5 sts rem, ending row with K2tog, K3; on WS rows, P3, P2tog, work across in patt as established until 5 sts rem in row, ending row with SSP, P3.
- **For fully-fashioned double decreases on front and back of sweater:** On RS rows, K3, SSSK, work across in patt as established until 6 sts rem, ending row with K3tog, K3; on WS rows, P3, P3tog, work across in patt as established until 6 sts rem in row, ending row with SSSP, P3.
- **For fully-fashioned single decreases on sleeves of sweater:** On RS rows, K1, SSK, work across in patt as established until 3 sts rem, ending row with K2tog, K1; on WS rows, P1, P2tog, work across in patt as established until 3 sts rem in row, ending row with SSP, P1.
- **For fully-fashioned double decreases on sleeves of sweater:** On RS rows, K1, SSSK, work across in patt as established until 4 sts rem, ending row with K3tog, K1; on WS rows, P1, P3tog, work across in patt as established until 4 sts rem in row, ending row with SSSP, P1.
- **For sweater assembly,** refer to the illustration for set-in construction on page 29.

Back
With smaller needles, CO 164 (188, 212, 236) sts.

Beg Cabled Rib Patt where indicated on chart, and work even for twenty-four rows.

Next Row (RS): Beg Main Cable Patt, and work even until piece measures approx 12½" from beg, ending after Row 16 of patt.

Shape Armholes
BO 9 (9, 18, 21) sts at beg of next two rows—146 (170, 176, 194) sts rem.

Work fully-fashioned double decreases each side every row 0 (6, 2, 6) times—146 (146, 168, 170) sts rem.

Work fully-fashioned single decreases each side every row 13 (16, 22, 25) times, then every other row 3 (0, 2, 0) times—114 (114, 120, 120) sts rem.

Maintaining 4 sts each side in Stockinette St Patt, cont even in patt until piece measures approx 20 (20½, 21, 21½)" from beg, ending after WS row.

Shape Shoulders
BO 6 (6, 7, 7) sts at beg of next six rows. BO 8 sts at beg of next two rows—62 sts rem.

BO.

Front
Work same as Back until piece measures approx 18 (18½, 19, 19½)" from beg, ending after WS row.

Shape Neck
Next Row (RS): Work across first 45 (45, 48, 48) sts; join second ball of yarn and BO middle 24 sts, work to end row.

Work both sides at once with separate balls of yarn, and BO 6 sts each neck edge once, then BO 4 sts each neck edge once—35 (35, 38, 38) sts rem each side.

Work both sides at once with separate balls of yarn, and dec 1 st each neck edge every row nine times—26 (26, 29, 29) sts rem each side.

Cont even, if necessary, until piece measures same as Back to shoulders.

Shape Shoulders
Work same as for Back.

Sleeves
With smaller needles, CO 84 sts.

Beg Cabled Rib Patt, and work even for twelve rows.

Next Row (RS): Beg Main Cable Patt, and inc 1 st each side every other row 0 (0, 8, 12) times, every fourth row 12 (24, 23, 21) times, then every sixth row 10 (2, 0, 0) times, working new sts in patt—128 (136, 146, 150) sts.

Cont even until piece measures approx 17¾ " from beg, ending after WS row.

Shape Cap
BO 9 (9, 19, 21) sts at beg of next two rows—110 (118, 110, 108) sts rem.

Work fully-fashioned double decreases each side every row 6 (3, 0, 0) times—86 (106, 110, 108) sts rem.

Work fully-fashioned single decreases each side every row 22 (32, 29, 24) times, then every other row 0 (0, 5, 9) times—42 sts rem.

BO 5 sts at beg of next four rows—22 sts rem.

BO.

Finishing
Block pieces (see "Blocking" on page 28) to measurements.

Sew left shoulder seam.

Neckband
With RS facing and smaller needles, pick up and knit 110 sts along neckline.

Beg where indicated on Cabled Rib Patt, and work Row 2 of chart, then work Rows 3-6 of chart.

Work Rows 1-6, then Rows 1 and 2 of Cabled Rib Patt.

Work Row 2 of chart once more, *switching WS to RS to allow RS of patt to show when turtleneck is folded over.*

Cont even in Cabled Rib Patt as established until neckband measures approx 4" from beg.

Change to larger needles, and cont even in patt as established until neckband measures approx 7¼" from beg.

BO *loosely* in patt.

Sew right shoulder seam, including side of neckband, reversing seam at same point as RS/WS switch in neckband.

Set in Sleeves. Sew sleeve and side seams.

CABLED RIB PATTERN

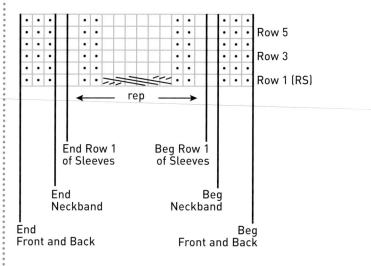

MAIN CABLE PATTERN

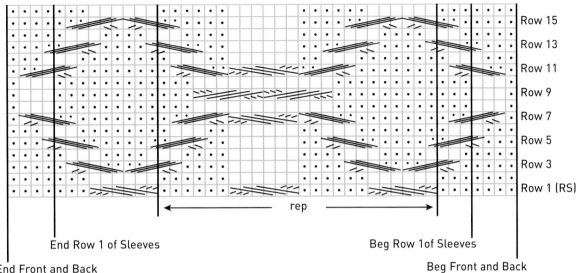

Row 15
Row 13
Row 11
Row 9
Row 7
Row 5
Row 3
Row 1 (RS)

rep

End Row 1 of Sleeves

Beg Row 1of Sleeves

End Front and Back

Beg Front and Back

PATTERN STITCH KEY

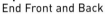

• = P on RS; K on WS

☐ = K on RS; P on WS

= Slip 3 sts onto cn and hold in front; K3; K3 from cn

= Slip 2 sts onto cn and hold in back; K3; P2 from cn

= Slip 3 sts onto cn and hold in front; P2; K3 from cn

= Slip 3 sts onto cn and hold in back; K3; K3 from cn

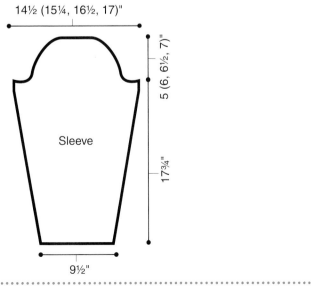

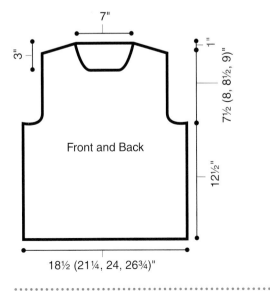

3"

7"

1"

7½ (8, 8½, 9)"

Front and Back

12½"

18½ (21¼, 24, 26¾)"

14½ (15¼, 16½, 17)"

5 (6, 6½, 7)"

Sleeve

17¾"

9½"

Sleeveless V-Neck

Here's my favorite kind of project! Nearly every right side row is different, so it's fun to watch the intricate pattern grow. Even the neckband and armbands are integrated, so finishing is a breeze.

Skill Level
Experienced

Sizes
Small (Medium, Large, 1X, 2X). Instructions are for smallest size, with changes for other sizes noted in parentheses as necessary.

Finished Measurements
Bust: 34 (37, 40, 43, 46½)"
Upper hip: 30½ (34, 36, 40, 43)"
Total length: 22¾"

Materials
- Muench Yarns/GGH's Goa (5-bulky weight; 50% cotton/50% acrylic; each approx 1¾ oz/50 g and 66 yd/60 m), 11 (13, 15, 17, 19) balls in #53 Lime
- One pair of size 10 (6 mm) knitting needles or size needed to obtain gauge
- One cable needle
- Two stitch markers
- One blunt-end yarn needle

Gauge
In Reverse Stockinette St Patt, 14 sts and 22 rows = 4".
To save time, take time to check gauge.

Stitch Patterns
Reverse Stockinette Stitch Pattern *(any number of sts)*
Row 1 (RS): Purl across.
Row 2: Knit across.
Repeat Rows 1 and 2 for patt.

Cable Rib Pattern *(66-st panel)*
See chart on page 93.

Main Cable Pattern *(66-st panel)*
See chart on page 93.

NOTES
- **For fully-fashioned increases:** On WS rows, K3, M1, work across until 3 sts rem, ending row with M1, K3.
- **For fully-fashioned armhole decreases:** On RS rows, K3, P3, K2, SSK, work across in patt as established until 10 sts rem, ending row with K2tog, K2, P3, K3; on WS rows, P3, K3, P2, P2tog, work across in patt as established until 10 sts rem in row, ending row with SSP, P2, K3, P3.
- **For fully-fashioned neckline decreases:** Work patt as established until 10 sts before center of sweater, slip next st onto cn and hold in back, K3, P1 from cn, P2, K2tog, K2; with second ball of yarn, K2, SSK, P2, slip next 3 sts onto cn and hold in front, P1, K3 from cn, work patts as established across to end row.
- **For ease in finishing,** instructions include one selvedge st each side; these sts are not included in final measurements.

Back
CO 82 (88, 92, 98, 104) sts.

Set Up Patts
Row 1 (RS): Work Row 1 of Reverse Stockinette St Patt across first 8 (11, 13, 16, 19) sts, place marker, work Row 1 of Cable Rib Patt over middle 66 sts, place marker, and work Row 1 of Reverse Stockinette St Patt across to end row.

Cont patts as established, and work fully-fashioned increases each side on next WS row and then every twentieth row two *more* times, beg Main Cable Patt when Row 30 of Cable Rib Patt is completed—88 (94, 98, 104, 110) sts.

Cont even in patts as established until piece measures approx 14¾ (14¾, 14½, 14½, 14¼)" from beg, ending after WS row.

Shape Armholes and Neck
Cont patts as established, work fully-fashioned armhole decreases each side every row 2 (4, 6, 10, 14) times, every other row 7 (10, 10, 10, 9) times, then every fourth row 3 (1, 1, 0, 0) times, **and at the same time,** when Row 54 of Main

Cable Patt is completed, place a marker on needle to indi-cate center of sweater, and work fully-fashioned neckline decreases on each side of neck every other row fourteen times, then every fourth row three times, maintaining cables as established as long as possible—15 sts rem.

Cont even in patts as established until piece measures approx 21¾" from beg, ending after WS row.

Shape Shoulders
BO 5 sts at beg of next six rows.

Front
Work same as Back.

Finishing
Block pieces (see "Blocking" on page 28) to measurements.

Sew shoulder seams.

Sew side seams.

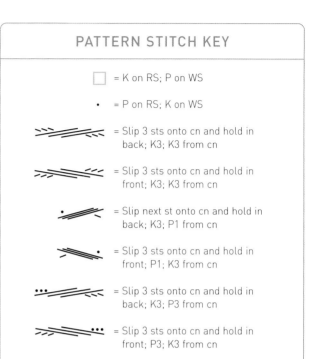

PATTERN STITCH KEY

☐ = K on RS; P on WS

• = P on RS; K on WS

= Slip 3 sts onto cn and hold in back; K3; K3 from cn

= Slip 3 sts onto cn and hold in front; K3; K3 from cn

= Slip next st onto cn and hold in back; K3; P1 from cn

= Slip 3 sts onto cn and hold in front; P1; K3 from cn

= Slip 3 sts onto cn and hold in back; K3; P3 from cn

= Slip 3 sts onto cn and hold in front; P3; K3 from cn

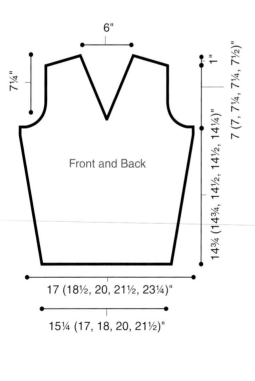

6"

7¼"

1"

7 (7, 7¼, 7¼, 7½)"

14¾ (14¾, 14½, 14¼, 14¼)"

Front and Back

17 (18½, 20, 21½, 23¼)"

15¼ (17, 18, 20, 21½)"

CABLE RIB PATTERN

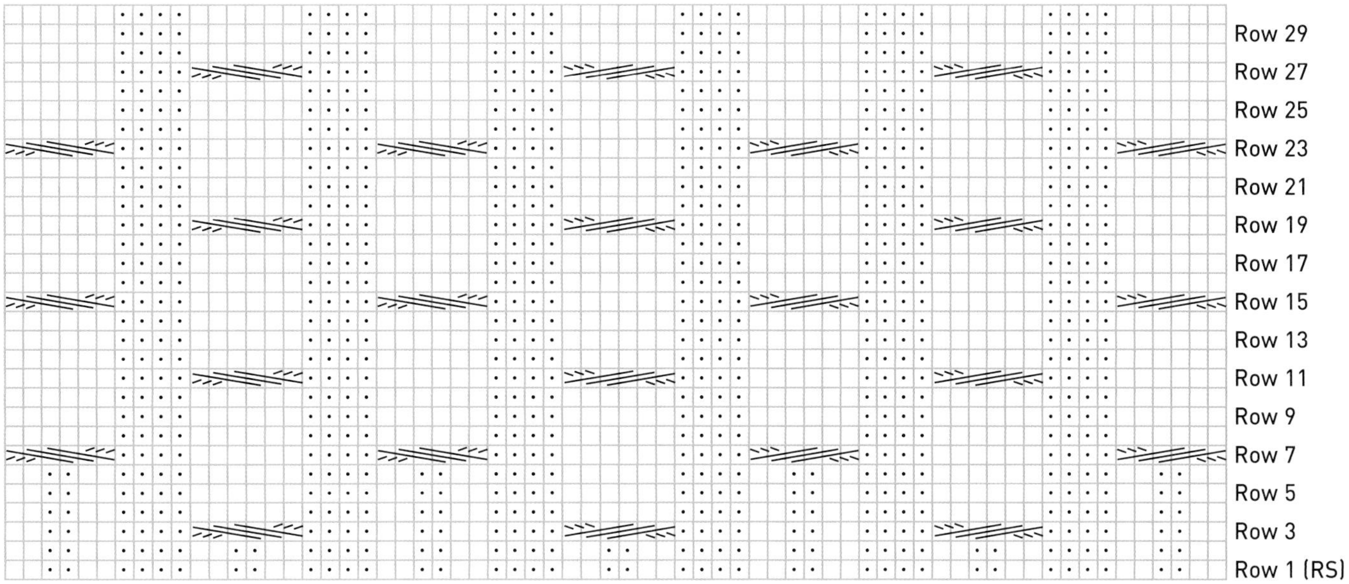

Row 29
Row 27
Row 25
Row 23
Row 21
Row 19
Row 17
Row 15
Row 13
Row 11
Row 9
Row 7
Row 5
Row 3
Row 1 (RS)

MAIN CABLE PATTERN

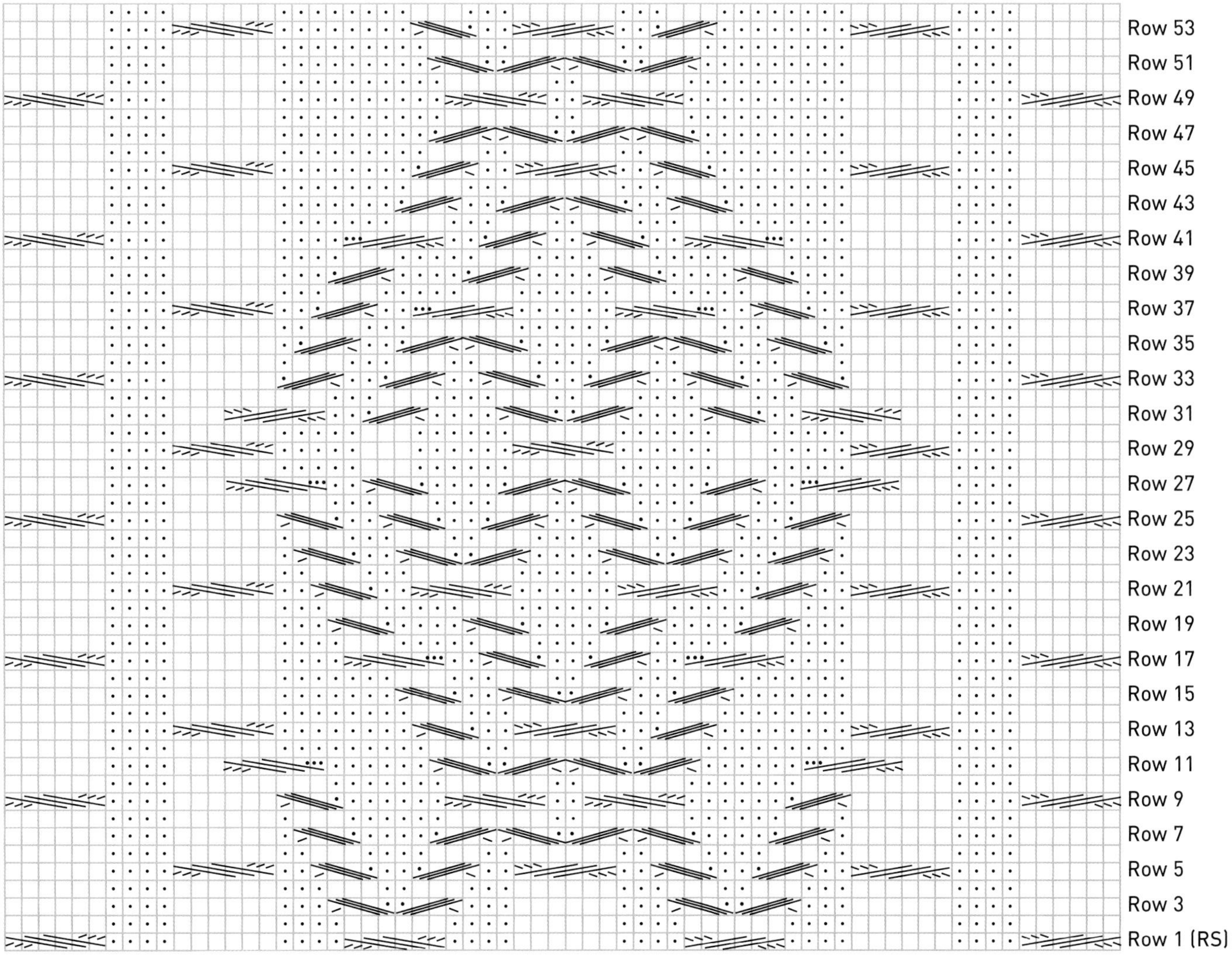

Row 53
Row 51
Row 49
Row 47
Row 45
Row 43
Row 41
Row 39
Row 37
Row 35
Row 33
Row 31
Row 29
Row 27
Row 25
Row 23
Row 21
Row 19
Row 17
Row 15
Row 13
Row 11
Row 9
Row 7
Row 5
Row 3
Row 1 (RS)

Chapter 5

Shower Them with Cables

···

GIFTS FOR YOUR LUCKY FRIENDS AND FAMILY

Classic and always in style, cabled projects make great gifts.
They're fun to create—and to receive! Knit a traditional crewneck
pullover for your niece or nephew, or whip up a cool handbag for your
favorite gal pal. The cotton-rich baby blanket, with its interesting
four-piece construction, is a joy to create. It'll make any mom happy.
For a larger project, make a tweed pullover for the special man in
your life. Be sure to choose a color that looks good on you, though.
Chances are you'll be borrowing it!

Man's Intertwined Cables Pullover

Intertwined cables cover this anything-but-basic pullover.
The integrated cabled ribbing adds the perfect finishing touch!

Skill Level
Intermediate

Sizes
Extra-Small (Small, Medium, Large, Extra-Large).
Instructions are for smallest size, with changes for other
sizes noted in parentheses as necessary.

Finished Measurements
Chest: 39 (44, 49, 54, 59)"
Total length: 24 (24½, 24½, 25, 25½)"

Materials
- Cascade Yarns's Cascade 220 (4-worsted weight;
  100% wool; each approx 3½ oz/100 g and 220 yd/201 m),
  9 (10, 10, 11, 11) hanks in #9322 Forest Heather
- One pair *each* of sizes 6 and 8 (4 and 5 mm) knitting
  needles or size needed to obtain gauge
- One cable needle
- One blunt-end yarn needle

Gauge
In Intertwined Cables Patt with larger needles, 26 sts and
27 rows = 4". **To save time, take time to check gauge.**

Stitch Patterns
Cable Rib Pattern *(mult 16 + 18 sts)*
See chart on page 99.

Intertwined Cables Pattern *(mult 16 + 18 sts)*
See chart on page 99.

NOTE
- **For sweater assembly**, refer to the illustration for
  square indented construction on page 29.
- **For a higher neckband,** just continue knitting until your
  band measures your desired height!

Back
With smaller needles, CO 130 (146, 162, 178, 194) sts.

Beg Cable Rib Patt, and work even until piece measures
approx 3" from beg, ending after Row 4 of patt.

Change to larger needles, beg Intertwined Cables Patt, and
work even until piece measures approx 13½" from beg,
ending after WS row.

Shape Armholes
BO 16 sts at beg of next two rows—98 (114, 130, 146, 162)
sts rem.

Cont even until piece measures approx 23 (23½, 23½, 24,
24½)" from beg, ending after WS row.

Shape Shoulders
BO 6 (8, 10, 12, 14) sts at beg of next six rows. BO 5 (7, 9,
11, 13) sts at beg of next two rows—52 sts rem.

BO.

Front
Work same as Back until piece measures approx 21 (21½,
21½, 22, 22½)" from beg, ending after WS row.

Shape Neck
Next Row (RS): Work across first 38 (46, 54, 62, 70) sts; join
second ball of yarn and BO middle 22 sts, work to end row.

Work both sides at once with separate balls of yarn, and
BO 4 sts each neck edge once, then BO 2 sts each neck
edge two times—30 (38, 46, 54, 62) sts rem each side.

Work both sides at once with separate balls of yarn, and
dec 1 st each neck edge every row seven times—23 (31, 39,
47, 55) sts rem each side.

Cont even, if necessary, until piece measures same as
Back to shoulders.

Shape Shoulders
Work same as for Back.

Sleeves

With smaller needles, CO 66 sts.

Beg Cable Rib Patt, and work even until piece measures approx 3" from beg, ending after Row 4 of patt.

Change to larger needles, beg Intertwined Cables Patt, and inc 1 st each side on next row and then every other row 0 (9, 11, 18, 28) times, then every fourth row 28 (22, 20, 16, 10) times—124 (130, 130, 136, 144) sts.

Cont even until piece measures approx 22½ (21¾, 21, 20¾, 20)" from beg.

BO.

Finishing

Block pieces (see "Blocking" on page 28) to measurements.

Sew left shoulder seam.

Neckband

With RS facing and smaller needles, pick up and knit 114 sts along neckline.

Beg Cable Rib Patt, and work even until neckband measures approx 1½" from beg, ending after Row 1 of patt.

BO *loosely* in patt.

Sew right shoulder seam.

Set in Sleeves. Sew sleeve and side seams.

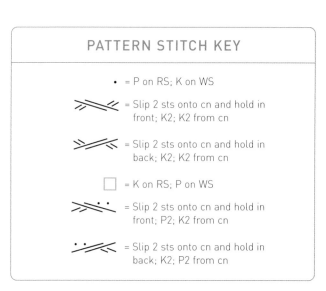

PATTERN STITCH KEY

- • = P on RS; K on WS
- = Slip 2 sts onto cn and hold in front; K2; K2 from cn
- = Slip 2 sts onto cn and hold in back; K2; K2 from cn
- □ = K on RS; P on WS
- = Slip 2 sts onto cn and hold in front; P2; K2 from cn
- = Slip 2 sts onto cn and hold in back; K2; P2 from cn

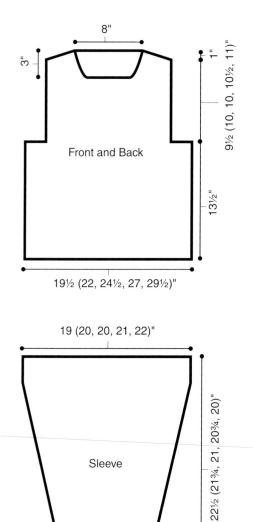

Front and Back

8"

3"

1"

9½ (10, 10, 10½, 11)"

13½"

19½ (22, 24½, 27, 29½)"

19 (20, 20, 21, 22)"

Sleeve

22½ (21¾, 21, 20¾, 20)"

10"

CABLE RIB PATTERN

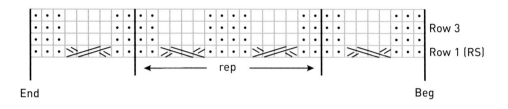

Row 3

Row 1 (RS)

← rep →

End

Beg

INTERTWINED CABLES PATTERN

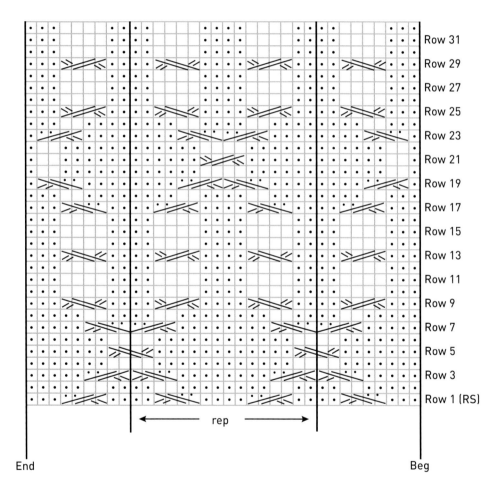

Row 31

Row 29

Row 27

Row 25

Row 23

Row 21

Row 19

Row 17

Row 15

Row 13

Row 11

Row 9

Row 7

Row 5

Row 3

Row 1 (RS)

← rep →

End

Beg

His/Hers Reversible Scarf

It might seem odd crossing cables on both right side and wrong side rows, but doing so creates a fabric that's completely reversible. It's not difficult to knit: just keep track of which row you're on at all times.

Skill Level
Easy

Size
One size

Finished Measurements
Approx 7 x 66"

Materials
- Blue Sky Alpaca's Worsted Hand Dyes (4-worsted weight; 50% alpaca/50% wool; each approx 3½ oz/100 g and 100 yd/91 m), 5 balls in #2000 Red
- One pair *each* of sizes 7 and 9 (4.5 and 5.5 mm) knitting needles or size needed to obtain gauge
- One cable needle
- One safety pin

Gauge
In Reversible Cable Patt, 21 sts and 21 rows = 4".
To save time, take time to check gauge.

Stitch Patterns
K6 P6 Rib Pattern (mult 12 sts)
Patt Row: *K6, P6. Repeat from * across.
Repeat Patt Row.

Reversible Cable Pattern (mult 12 sts)
See chart below.

SCARF
With smaller needles, CO 48 sts.

Beg K6 P6 Rib Patt, and work even for four rows total.

Next Row (RS): Change to larger needles, and beg Reversible Cable Patt. Mark this side of fabric with a safety pin as an odd-numbered row.

Cont even in Reversible Cable Patt until piece measures approx 65½" from beg, ending after Row 6 of patt.

Next Row (RS): Change to smaller needles, and work K6 P6 Rib Patt for four rows total.

BO in rib.

Block (see "Blocking" on page 28) to measurements.

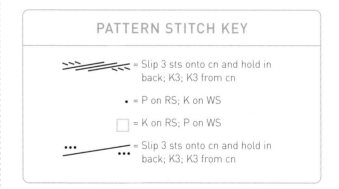

PATTERN STITCH KEY

= Slip 3 sts onto cn and hold in back; K3; K3 from cn

• = P on RS; K on WS

□ = K on RS; P on WS

= Slip 3 sts onto cn and hold in back; K3; K3 from cn

REVERSIBLE CABLE PATTERN

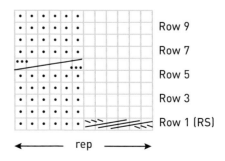

Row 9
Row 7
Row 5
Row 3
Row 1 (RS)

← rep →

Little Bag with Handles

You'll be surprised at how fast you can make this funky bag.
Good thing, because everyone you know is going to want one!

Skill Level
Intermediate

Size
One size

Finished Measurements
Approx 9½" wide x 9" deep

Materials
- Classic Elite Yarns's Bazic (4-worsted weight; 100% superwash wool; each approx 1¾ oz/50 g and 65 yd/59 m), 3 balls in #2985 Marigold
- One pair of size 9 (5.5 mm) knitting needles or size needed to obtain gauge
- One cable needle
- Two stitch markers
- One blunt-end yarn needle
- Two pieces of Judi and Company's Plastic Purse Handles, Style #PL-10, 5" square, in Pumpkin
- [Optional: fabric for lining]

Gauge
In Stockinette St Patt, 18 sts and 24 rows = 4".
To save time, take time to check gauge.

Stitch Patterns

Stockinette St Pattern *(any number of sts)*
Row 1 (RS): Knit across.
Row 2: Purl across.
Repeat Rows 1 and 2 for patt.

Cable Panel *(33-st panel)*
See chart on page 103.

Seed St Pattern *(mult 2 + 1 sts)*
Row 1 (WS): *K1, P1. Repeat from * across, ending row with K1.
Patt Row: As Row 1.
Repeat Patt Row for patt.

NOTE
- **For ease in finishing,** instructions include one selvedge st each side; these sts are not reflected in final mea-surements.

Back
CO 55 sts.

Set Up Patts
Work Row 1 of Stockinette St Patt over first st, place marker, work Row 1 of Cable Panel over next 33 sts, place marker, work Row 1 of Stockinette St Patt across to end row.

Work even in patts as established for three more rows.

Next Row (RS): Work Stockinette St Patt as established to first marker, M1, work Cable Panel as established across to next marker, SSK, work Stockinette St as established across to end row—55 sts.

Cont patts as established, and repeat last row every other row eighteen times.

Cont even in patts as established for four rows.

Next Row (RS): Beg Seed St Patt, and dec 27 sts evenly across—28 sts rem.

Cont even in Seed St Patt until piece measures approx 10½" from beg.

BO.

Front

Work same as Back.

Finishing

Block pieces (see "Blocking" on page 28) to measurements.

Sew sides and bottom of bag, leaving upper 4¼" unsewn on both sides.

Fold Seed Stitch Patt portion of one piece around one handle, and sew into place.

Repeat for second piece.

[Optional: Cut fabric to fit inside of bag plus ¼" selvedge on all sides. Sew lining into place.]

PATTERN STITCH KEY

☐ = K on RS; P on WS

• = P on RS; K on WS

= Slip 2 sts onto cn and hold in back; K1; K2 from cn

= Slip 3 sts onto cn and hold in front; K3; K3 from cn

= Slip 3 sts onto cn and hold in back; K3; K3 from cn

= Slip next st onto cn and hold in front; K2; K1 from cn

CABLE PANEL

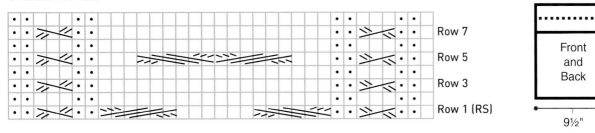

Row 7

Row 5

Row 3

Row 1 (RS)

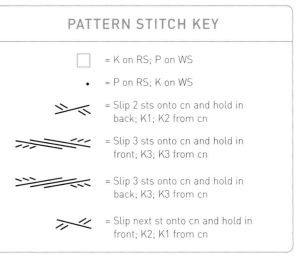

Front and Back

3"

7½"

9½"

Child's Crewneck Pullover

Several interesting cabled panels are featured in this design: twisted stitches that zig and zag, vertical braids, and a beautiful central panel that's comprised of entwined hearts.

Skill Level
Intermediate

Sizes
Child's size 2 (4, 6, 8). Instructions are for smallest size, with changes for other sizes noted in parentheses as necessary.

Finished Measurements
Chest: 26 (29, 31½, 34)"
Total length: 14 (15, 16, 17)"

Materials
- Westminster Fibers/Jaeger's Baby Merino DK (3-DK weight; 100% wool; each approx 1¾ oz/50 g and 130 yd/120 m), 7 (7, 8, 9) balls in #227 Rose
- One pair *each* of sizes 4 and 5 (3.5 and 3.75 mm) knitting needles or size needed to obtain gauge
- One cable needle
- Three stitch markers
- One blunt-end yarn needle

Gauge
In Box St Patt with larger needles, 26 sts and 34 rows = 4".
To save time, take time to check gauge.

Stitch Patterns
Twisted Rib Pattern *(mult 2 + 1 sts)*
Row 1 (RS): *K next st *through back loop*, P1. Repeat from * across, ending row with K next st *through back loop*.
Row 2: *P next st *through back loop*, K1. Repeat from * across, ending row with P next st *through back loop*.
Repeat Rows 1 and 2 for patt.

Box Stitch Pattern *(mult 4 + 2 sts)*
Row 1 (RS): *K2, P2. Repeat from * across, ending row with K2.
Row 2: *P2, K2. Repeat from * across, ending row with P2.
Row 3: As Row 2.
Row 4: As Row 1.
Repeat Rows 1-4 for patt.

Right Cable Pattern
See chart on page 107.

Left Cable Pattern
See chart on page 107.

NOTE
- **For sweater assembly,** refer to the illustration for square indented saddle-shoulder construction on page 29.

Back
With smaller needles, CO 95 (103, 111, 119) sts.

Beg Twisted Rib Patt and work even until piece measures approx 1½" from beg, ending after RS row.

Next Row (WS): Cont patt as established, and work across first 15 (19, 23, 27) sts, M1, work 2 sts, M1, work 3 sts, M1, work 6 sts, M1, work 14 sts, M1, work 3 sts, M1, work 4 sts, M1, (work 2 sts, M1) two times, work 4 sts, M1, work 2 sts, M1, work 14 sts, M1, work 7 sts, M1, (work 2 sts, M1) two times, (work 5 sts, M1) two times, work across to end row—112 (120, 128, 136) sts.

Change to larger needles, work Row 1 of Box St Patt over first 10 (14, 18, 22) sts, place marker, work Row 1 of Right Cable Patt over next 46 sts, place marker, work Left Cable Patt over next 46 sts, place marker, work Row 1 of Box St Patt to end row.

Cont even in patts as established until piece measures approx 8½ (9, 9½, 10)" from beg, ending after WS row.

Shape Armholes
BO 4 (8, 8, 12) sts at beg of next two rows—104 (104, 112, 112) sts rem.

Cont even until piece measures approx 12¼ (13¼, 14¼, 15¼)" from beg, ending after WS row. BO.

Front

Work same as Back until piece measures approx 11¾ (12¾, 13¾, 14¾)" from beg, ending after WS row.

Shape Neck

Next Row (RS): Work across first 36 (36, 37, 37) sts; join second ball of yarn and BO middle 32 (32, 38, 38) sts, work to end row.

Work both sides at once with separate balls of yarn, and BO 4 sts each neck edge once, then dec 1 st each neck edge every row once—31 (31, 32, 32) sts rem each side.

Cont even until piece measures same as Back. BO.

Sleeves

With smaller needles, CO 57 (57, 67, 67) sts.

Beg Twisted Rib Patt, and work even until piece measures approx 1½" from beg, ending after RS row.

For Sizes 2 and 4 Only

Next Row: Cont patt as established, and work across first 6 sts, M1, work 14 sts, M1, work 2 sts, M1, work 4 sts, M1, (work 2 sts, M1) two times, work 4 sts, M1, work 3 sts, M1, work 14 sts, M1, work across to end row—66 sts.

For Sizes 6 and 8 Only

Next Row: Cont patt as established, and work across first 2 sts, M1, work across 2 sts, M1, work across 7 sts, M1, work 14 sts, M1, work 2 sts, M1, work 4 sts, M1, (work 2 sts, M1) two times, work 4 sts, M1, work 3 sts, M1, work 14 sts, M1, work 6 sts, M1, work across 3 sts, M1, work across to end row—80 sts.

For All Sizes

Change to larger needles, beg Row 1 of Right Cable Patt where indicated, then work Row 1 of Left Cable Patt where indicated to end row.

Cont patts as established, and work even for two rows.

Cont patts as established, and inc 1 st each side on next row and then every fourth row 7 (12, 0, 3) more times, every sixth row 7 (5, 11, 13) times, then every eighth row 0 (0, 2, 0) times, working new sts into Right and Left Cable Patts as they accumulate. When all Right and Left Cable sts on charts have been added, work rem new sts in Box St Patt—96 (102, 108, 114) sts.

Cont even until piece measures approx 11½ (12¾, 13½, 15)" from beg.

Shape Saddle

BO 31 (34, 37, 40) sts at beg of next two rows—34 sts rem.

Cont even in patts as established until saddle measures approx 3½ (3½, 3¾, 3¾)" from beg. BO.

Finishing

Block pieces (see "Blocking" on page 28) to measurements.

Set in Sleeves, leaving left back shoulder seam unsewn.

Neck Edging

With RS facing and smaller needles, pick up and K 120 (120, 124, 124) sts along neckline.

Row 1 (WS): *K1, P next st *through back loop*. Repeat from * across.

Row 2: *P1, K next st *through back loop*. Repeat from * across. Repeat last two rows until neckband measures approx 1" from beg. BO *loosely* in patt.

Sew left shoulder seam, including side of neckband.

Sew sleeve and side seams.

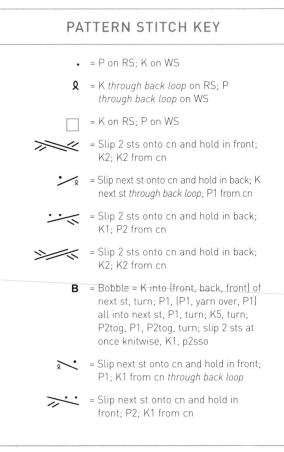

PATTERN STITCH KEY

- **·** = P on RS; K on WS
- **ℓ** = K *through back loop* on RS; P *through back loop* on WS
- **□** = K on RS; P on WS
- = Slip 2 sts onto cn and hold in front; K2; K2 from cn
- = Slip next st onto cn and hold in back; K next st *through back loop*; P1 from cn
- = Slip 2 sts onto cn and hold in back; K1; P2 from cn
- = Slip 2 sts onto cn and hold in back; K2; K2 from cn
- **B** = Bobble = K into (front, back, front) of next st, turn; P1, (P1, yarn over, P1) all into next st, P1, turn; K5, turn; P2tog, P1, P2tog, turn; slip 2 sts at once knitwise, K1, p2sso
- = Slip next st onto cn and hold in front; P1; K1 from cn *through back loop*
- = Slip next st onto cn and hold in front; P2; K1 from cn

RIGHT CABLE PATTERN

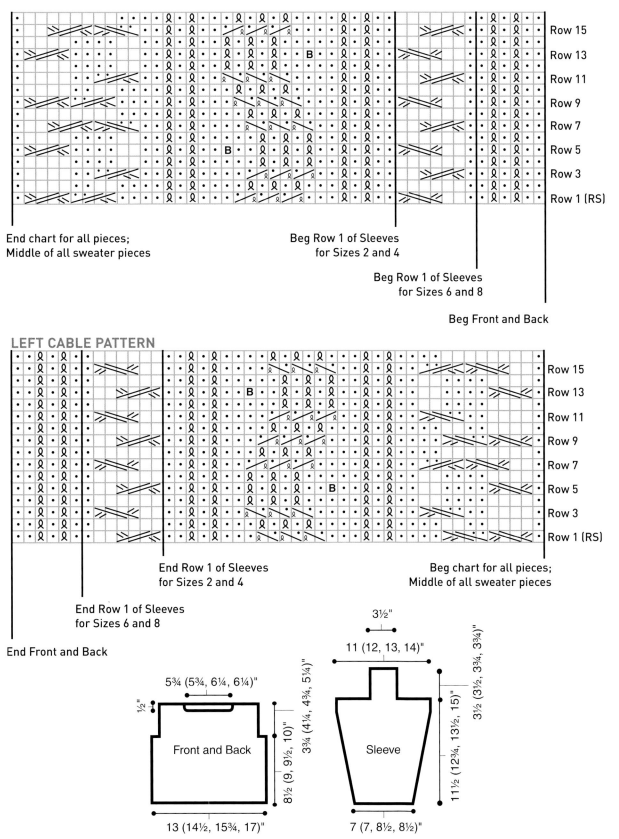

Row 15
Row 13
Row 11
Row 9
Row 7
Row 5
Row 3
Row 1 (RS)

End chart for all pieces;
Middle of all sweater pieces

Beg Row 1 of Sleeves
for Sizes 2 and 4

Beg Row 1 of Sleeves
for Sizes 6 and 8

Beg Front and Back

LEFT CABLE PATTERN

Row 15
Row 13
Row 11
Row 9
Row 7
Row 5
Row 3
Row 1 (RS)

End Row 1 of Sleeves
for Sizes 2 and 4

Beg chart for all pieces;
Middle of all sweater pieces

End Row 1 of Sleeves
for Sizes 6 and 8

End Front and Back

3½"

11 (12, 13, 14)"

3½ (3½, 3¾, 3¾)"

5¾ (5¾, 6¼, 6¼)"

3¾ (4¼, 4¾, 5¼)"

½"

Front and Back

Sleeve

11½ (12¾, 13½, 15)"

8½ (9, 9½, 10)"

13 (14½, 15¾, 17)"

7 (7, 8½, 8½)"

Man's Tweed Pullover

I'll bet you'll want to knit this casual saddle-shoulder sweater
for your guy just so you can borrow it!

Skill Level
Experienced

Sizes
Extra-Small (Small, Medium, Large, Extra-Large).
Instructions are for smallest size, with changes for other
sizes noted in parentheses as necessary.

Finished Measurements
Chest: 39½ (45½, 51½, 57½, 63½)"
Total length: 26 (27, 27½, 27½, 27½)"

Materials
- Westminster Fibers/Rowan's Yorkshire Tweed DK (3-DK
  weight; 100% wool; each approx 1¾ oz/50 g and 123
  yd/113 m), 15 (16, 17, 18, 19) balls in #349 Frog
- One pair of size 6 (4 mm) knitting needles or size needed
  to obtain gauge
- One cable needle
- Eight stitch markers
- One blunt-end yarn needle

Gauge
Each 13-st panel of Narrow Panel measures 2⅛" across;
each 22-st panel of Wide Panel measures 2¾" wide; and 28
rows = 4" tall. **To save time, take time to check gauge.**

Stitch Patterns
Cabled Rib Pattern *(mult 4 sts)*
See chart on page 111.

Right-Edge Pattern *(mult 9 sts)*
See chart on page 111.

Narrow Panel *(13-st panel)*
See chart on page 111.

Wide Panel *(22-st panel)*
See chart on page 111.

Left-Edge Pattern *(mult 9 sts)*
See chart on page 111.

NOTE
- **For sweater assembly,** refer to the illustration for
  square indented saddle-shoulder construction on
  page 29.

Back
CO 124 (140, 156, 172, 188) sts.

Beg Cabled Rib Patt, and work even until piece measures
approx 2½" from beg, ending after RS row.

Next Row (WS): Cont patt as established, and [work across
first 8 sts, M1] 1 (2, 3, 4, 5) times, work across next 7 sts,
M1, [work across next 16 sts, M1, work across next 4 sts,
M1, work across next 12 sts, M1] three times, work across
next 5 sts, [M1, work across next 8 sts] 1 (2, 3, 4, 5) times
to end row—136 (154, 172, 190, 208) sts.

Set Up Patts
Next Row (RS): Work Row 1 of Right-Edge Patt over 9 (18, 27,
36, 45) sts, place marker, [work Row 1 of Narrow Panel over
next 13 sts, place marker, work Row 1 of Wide Panel over
next 22 sts, place marker] three times, work Row 1 of Narrow
Panel over next 13 sts, place marker, work Row 1 of Left-
Edge Patt over 9 (18, 27, 36, 45) sts to end row.

Cont even in patts as established until piece measures approx
15½ (16½, 15¾, 15¾, 15¾)" from beg, ending after WS row.

Shape Armholes
BO 13 (18, 18, 27, 27) sts at beg of next two rows—110
(118, 136, 136, 154) sts rem.

Cont even until piece measures approx 23 (24, 24½, 24½,
24½)" from beg, ending after WS row.

Shape Shoulders
BO 7 (8, 11, 11, 13) sts at beg of next six rows, then BO 8 (9, 9, 9, 12) sts at beg of next two rows—52 sts rem.

BO.

Front
Work same as Back until piece measures approx 21 (22, 22½, 22½, 22½)" from beg, ending after WS row.

Shape Neck
Next Row (RS): Work across first 46 (50, 59, 59, 68) sts; join second ball of yarn and BO middle 18 sts, work to end row.

Work both sides at once with separate balls of yarn, and BO 6 sts each neck edge two times—34 (38, 47, 47, 56) sts rem each side.

Dec 1 st each neck edge every row three times, then every other row two times—29 (33, 42, 42, 51) sts rem each side.

Cont even, if necessary, until piece measures same as Back.

Shape Shoulders
Work same as for Back.

BO.

Sleeves
CO 60 sts.

Beg Cabled Rib Patt, and work even until piece measures approx 2½" from beg, ending after RS row.

Next Row (WS): Cont patt as established, and work across first 8 sts, M1, work across the next 7 sts, M1, work across the next 16 sts, M1, work across the next 4 sts, M1, work across the next 12 sts, M1, work across the next 5 sts, M1, work across the next 8 sts to end row—66 sts.

Set Up Patts
Next Row (RS): Work Row 1 of Right-Edge Patt over first 9 sts, place marker, work Row 1 of Narrow Panel over next 13 sts, place marker, work Row 1 of Wide Panel over next 22 sts, place marker, work Row 1 of Narrow Panel over next 13 sts, place marker, work Row 1 of Left-Edge Patt over 9 sts to end row.

Cont patts as established, and inc 1 st each side on next row and then every other row 0 (0, 8, 5, 8) times, every fourth row 14 (14, 27, 30, 27) times, then every sixth row 12 (12, 0, 0, 0) times, working new sts into Right-Edge Patt or Left-Edge Patt depending on which side of fabric they're on—120 (120, 138, 138, 138) sts.

Cont even until piece measures approx 22½ (22½, 21½, 22½, 21½)" from beg.

Shape Saddle
BO 45 (45, 54, 54, 54) sts at beg of next two rows—30 sts rem.

Cont even in patts as established until saddle measures approx 4 (4½, 6, 6, 7½)" from beg.

BO.

Finishing
Block pieces (see "Blocking" on page 28) to measurements.

Set in Sleeves, leaving left back shoulder seam unsewn.

Neck Edging
With RS facing, pick up and knit 134 sts along neckline.

Next Row (WS): P1, work Row 2 of Cabled Rib Patt across next 132 sts, ending row P1.

Next Row: K1, work Row 1 of Cabled Rib Patt across next 132 sts, ending row with K1.

Repeat last two rows until band measures approx 1¼" from beg, ending after WS row.

BO in patt.

Sew left shoulder seam.

Sew sleeve and side seams.

RIGHT-EDGE PATTERN

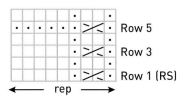

Row 5
Row 3
Row 1 (RS)

← rep →

NARROW PANEL

Row 5
Row 3
Row 1 (RS)

WIDE PANEL

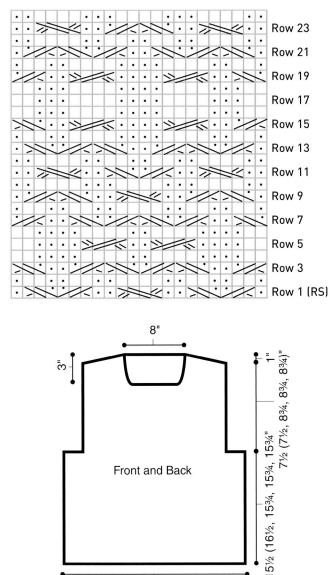

Row 23
Row 21
Row 19
Row 17
Row 15
Row 13
Row 11
Row 9
Row 7
Row 5
Row 3
Row 1 (RS)

Front and Back

8"

3"

19¾ (22¾, 25¾, 28¾, 31¾)"

15½ (16½, 15¾, 15¾, 15¾)"

7½ (7½, 8¾, 8¾, 8¾)"

1"

PATTERN STITCH KEY

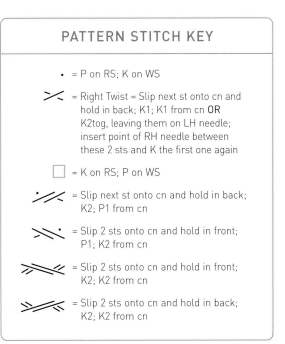

• = P on RS; K on WS

⋉ = Right Twist = Slip next st onto cn and hold in back; K1; K1 from cn OR K2tog, leaving them on LH needle; insert point of RH needle between these 2 sts and K the first one again

☐ = K on RS; P on WS

= Slip next st onto cn and hold in back; K2; P1 from cn

= Slip 2 sts onto cn and hold in front; P1; K2 from cn

= Slip 2 sts onto cn and hold in front; K2; K2 from cn

= Slip 2 sts onto cn and hold in back; K2; K2 from cn

LEFT-EDGE PATTERN

Row 5
Row 3
Row 1 (RS)

← rep →

CABLED RIB PATTERN

Row 1 (RS)

← rep →

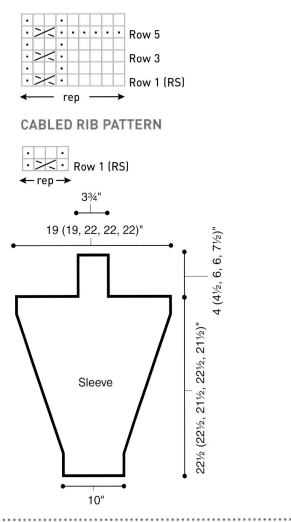

Sleeve

3¾"

19 (19, 22, 22, 22)"

10"

4 (4½, 6, 6, 7½)"

22½ (22½, 21½, 22½, 21½)"

Baby Blankie

Tired of knitting the same ol' one-piece baby afghan? Next time, try this one instead.
It's knit in four triangular sections that are sewn together to form a square.

Skill Level
Experienced

Finished Measurements
Approx 36 x 36"

Materials
- JCA/Reynolds's Cabana (5-bulky weight; 65% cotton/35% acrylic; each approx 3½ oz/100 g and 135 yds/123 m), 10 balls in #936 Soft Yellow
- One size 10 (6 mm) circular knitting needle, 16" long, or size needed to obtain gauge
- One cable needle
- One blunt-end yarn needle

Gauge
In Braid and Seed Stitch Patt, 19 sts and 20 rows = 4".
To save time, take time to check gauge.

Stitch Pattern
Braid and Seed Stitch Pattern
See chart on page 113.

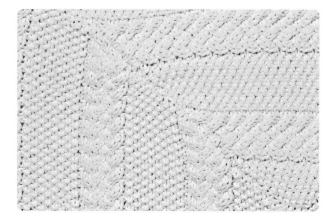

NOTES
- **Constructionwise,** this design is made in four triangular pieces; each triangle begins with a single st and then inc on one side until the required number of sts are added; sts are then dec on one side until a single st remains.
- **To simplify the printed instructions,** Rows 1-8 of the triangle are written out in words; after Row 8 is completed, cont working Braid and Seed St Patt as established, adding new sts into patt as soon as possible.

- **When knitting the shaped edge,** inc are only worked at the *end* of specified RS rows and at the *beg* of specified WS rows; to inc, K into the front and back of a st; to dec, K2tog.

Triangle
(Make four)
CO 1 st.

Begin Increases
Row 1 (RS): Knit into the front and back of st—2 sts.
Row 2: Knit into the front and back of first st, K1—3 sts.
Row 3: K1, P1, knit into the front and back of next st—4 sts.
Row 4: Knit into the front and back of first st, K1, P1, K1—5 sts.
Row 5: (K1, P1) two times, knit into the front and back of next st—6 sts.
Row 6: Knit into the front and back of first st, (K1, P1) two times, K1—7 sts.
Row 7: (K1, P1) three times, knit into the front and back of next st—8 sts.
Row 8: Knit into the front and back of first st, (K1, P1) three times, K1—9 sts.
Rows 9-75: Continue inc on shaped edge every row (see Notes), working Braid and Seed St Patt as established and adding new sts into patt as soon as possible—76 sts.
Next Two Rows (Rows 76 and 77): Work even in patt as established.
Next Five Rows (Rows 78-82): Inc on shaped edge every row—81 sts.
Next Row (Row 83): Work even in patt as established.
Next Five Rows (Rows 84-88): Inc on shaped edge every row—86 sts.
Next Two Rows (Rows 89 and 90): Work even in patt as established.
Next Five Rows (Rows 91-95): Inc on shaped edge *on RS rows only*—89 sts.
Next Seven Rows (Rows 96-102): Work even in patt as established.

Begin Decreases (see Notes)
Next Eight Rows (Rows 103-110): Dec on shaped edge *on RS rows only*—85 sts rem.
Next Five Rows (Rows 111-115): Dec on shaped edge every row—80 sts rem.
Next Row (Row 116): Work even in patt as established.
Next Five Rows (Rows 117-121): Dec on shaped edge every row—75 sts rem.

Next Row (Row 122): Work even in patt as established.
Rows 123-196: Dec on shaped edge every row—1 st rem.

BO.

Finishing
Block pieces (see "Blocking" on page 28) to measurements.

With RS facing, use Mattress St (see "Mattress Stitch Seam" on page 28) to join triangles, being careful to line up patt as seen in photograph.

PATTERN STITCH KEY

☐ = K on RS; P on WS

• = P on RS; K on WS

⤨ = Slip 2 sts onto cn and hold in back; K2; K2 from cn

⤨ = Slip 2 sts onto cn and hold in front; K2; K2 from cn

BRAID AND SEED STITCH PATTERN

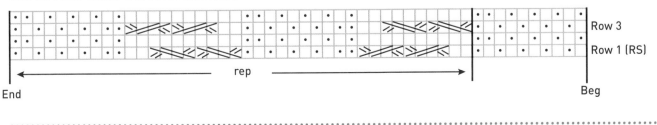

Row 3

Row 1 (RS)

rep

End

Beg

STITCH DICTIONARY

Cable Stitch Pattern Dictionary

Comprised of the two basic stitches—knit and purl—the sheer number and variety of cable stitch patterns possible is astounding. Here's a collection of more than 120 cables, from simple to complex. Many are traditional patterns passed on from generation to generation; others are original, designed especially for this book.

Whether you swap one cable called for in a particular project for another or design an entirely new item from one of these stitch patterns, I hope you'll find this section useful and inspirational.

HOW TO USE THE CABLE STITCH PATTERN DICTIONARY

This cable stitch pattern dictionary consists of three parts: Ribs, Panels, and Allover patterns.

Cabled Ribs

Cabled Ribs are patterns with a vertical alignment of knit and purl stitches. This arrangement of stitches creates fabrics that are especially stretchy with non-curling lower edges, making them particularly useful for the bottom borders of garments.

Cabled Panels

Cable Panels are isolated vertical cable designs placed on a plain background. Each panel is beautiful alone and also in combination with others.

Allover Cables

The Allover Cabled patterns are lush with texture and are suitable for a variety of projects. In these patterns, knit and purl stitches are scattered across the width of the fabric, often creating intricate designs.

Each of the three sections is arranged according to pattern width, from smallest to largest, and then by row repeat.

USING THE CABLE STITCH PATTERNS

To use one of these stitch patterns, knit a swatch at least two stitch repeats wide. Follow the chart until you've worked through the chart at least twice lengthwise, and then measure your gauge. When working with cable patterns, it can be difficult to count your stitches since some stitches are traveling behind others. Since you can't see all of the stitches to count them, simply measure one stitch repeat across and then divide by the number of stitches involved to find the gauge.

If you plan to wash and block your project pieces, it's important to take the time to treat your gauge swatch in the same manner *before* measuring it. Yarn often behaves differently after washing. Some fibers become limp while others bloom; some will contract lengthwise or widthwise. Consider your gauge swatch the perfect opportunity to preview a tiny piece of your completed project.

To check the gauge of a swatch of Allover 8, for example, cast on at least twenty-six stitches. Repeat Rows 1-12 of the chart at least twice, and then bind off.

Lay your swatch flat and measure its width, beginning from the left-hand edge of one Left Cross in Row 7 to the right-hand edge of the adjacent one—one complete stitch repeat. If that measurement is, say, 2", then your stitch gauge is eight stitches divided by 2", or four stitches to the inch.

If, on the other hand, you're using thicker yarn, the width of those same eight stitches might be 3½", so your stitch gauge would be eight stitches divided by 3½", or about two-and-one-quarter stitches to the inch. *Do not round this number—fractional inches add up when factored over an entire piece of fabric!*

If you're using several panels or stitch patterns within a single project, knit a separate gauge swatch for each of the panels or stitch patterns. Draw a rough sketch of your project, including the location of each cabled section.

Multiply your stitch gauge by the desired width of your fabric, and off you go! Of course, you might have to change your final width measurement a little in order to accommodate the stitch multiple for your particular stitch pattern. Keep in mind that knitwear design and pattern drafting are more of an art form than an exact science.

Enjoy yourself—and the seemingly infinite world of cables!

CABLING UP CLOSE

You can use schematic illustrations of pattern pieces such as those found in this book as size guidelines for specific projects or else draw shapes of your own.

Cabled Ribs

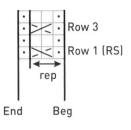

Row 3
Row 1 (RS)
rep

End   Beg

• = P on RS; K on WS

>< = Left Twist = Slip next st onto cn and hold in front; K1; K1 from cn **OR** skip first st and K next st *in back loop*; then K the skipped st; slip both sts off LH needle together

☐ = K on RS; P on WS

>< = Right Twist = Slip next st onto cn and hold in back; K1; K1 from cn **OR** K2tog, leaving them on LH needle; insert point of RH needle between these 2 sts and K the first one again

RIB 1
(mult 3 + 1 sts)

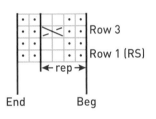

Row 3
Row 1 (RS)
← rep →

End   Beg

• = P on RS; K on WS

☐ = K on RS; P on WS

>< = Left Twist = Slip next st onto cn and hold in front; K1; K1 from cn **OR** skip first st and K next st *in back loop*; then K the skipped st; slip both sts off LH needle together

RIB 2
(mult 4 + 2 sts)

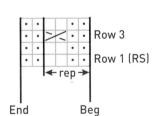

Row 3
Row 1 (RS)
← rep →

End   Beg

• = P on RS; K on WS

☐ = K on RS; P on WS

>< = Right Twist = Slip next st onto cn and hold in back; K1; K1 from cn **OR** K2tog, leaving them on LH needle; insert point of RH needle between these 2 sts and K the first one again

RIB 3
(mult 4 + 2 sts)

LEFT: Cable Rib patterns (clockwise from top left): 12, 1, 2, 7, 9, 8, 22, and 11

RIB 4
(mult of 5 + 1 sts)

• = P on RS; K on WS

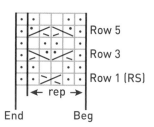

⤬ = Right Twist = Slip next st onto cn and hold in back; K1; K1 from cn **OR** K2tog, leaving them on LH needle; insert point of RH needle between these 2 sts and K the first one again

☐ = K on RS; P on WS

⤬ = Slip next st onto cn and hold in back; K1; P1 from cn

⤬ = Slip next st onto cn and hold in front; P1; K1 from cn

Row 5
Row 3
Row 1 (RS)
← rep →
End   Beg

RIB 5
(mult 5 + 2 sts)

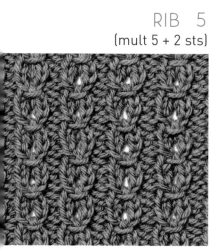

• = P on RS; K on WS

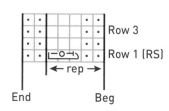

⌐o¬ = Slip the third st on LH needle over the first 2 sts as if to BO; K the first st; yarn over; then K the second st

☐ = K on RS; P on WS

Row 3
Row 1 (RS)
← rep →
End   Beg

RIB 6
(mult 5 + 2 sts)

• = P on RS; K on WS

| = Slip st purlwise with yarn in back on RS rows; slip st purlwise with yarn in front on WS rows

☐ = K on RS; P on WS

⤬ = Slip next st onto cn and hold in front; K2; K1 from cn

⤬ = Slip 2 sts onto cn and hold in back; K1; K2 from cn

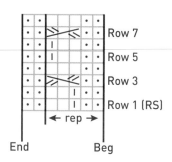

Row 7
Row 5
Row 3
Row 1 (RS)
← rep →
End   Beg

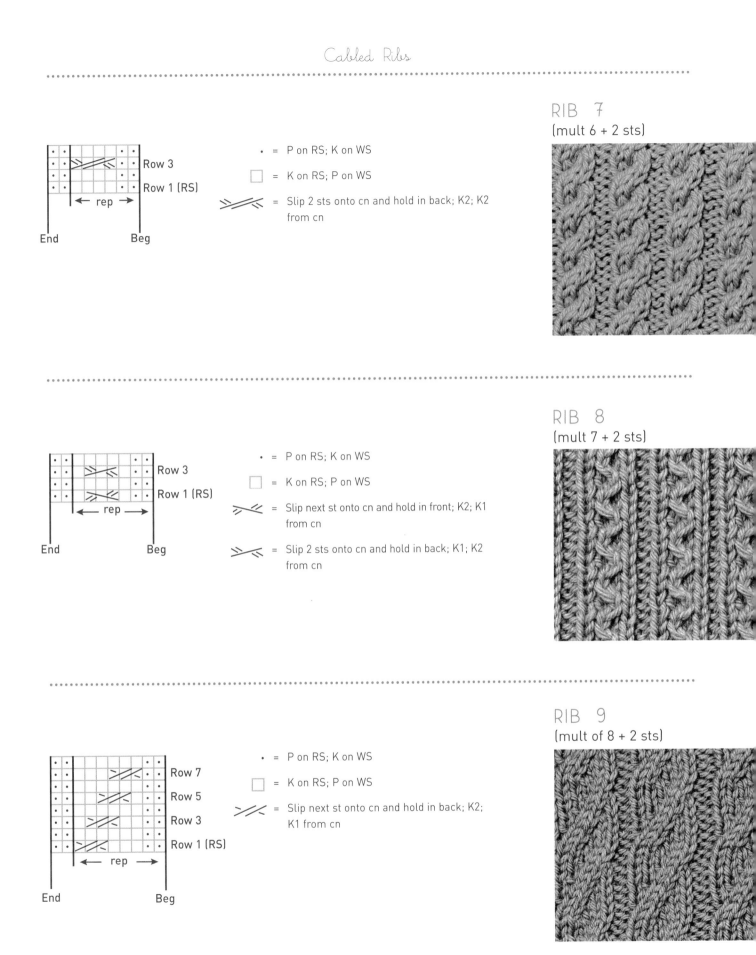

RIB 7
(mult 6 + 2 sts)

Row 3
Row 1 (RS)

← rep →

End   Beg

• = P on RS; K on WS

☐ = K on RS; P on WS

= Slip 2 sts onto cn and hold in back; K2; K2 from cn

RIB 8
(mult 7 + 2 sts)

Row 3
Row 1 (RS)

← rep →

End   Beg

• = P on RS; K on WS

☐ = K on RS; P on WS

= Slip next st onto cn and hold in front; K2; K1 from cn

= Slip 2 sts onto cn and hold in back; K1; K2 from cn

RIB 9
(mult of 8 + 2 sts)

Row 7
Row 5
Row 3
Row 1 (RS)

← rep →

End   Beg

• = P on RS; K on WS

☐ = K on RS; P on WS

= Slip next st onto cn and hold in back; K2; K1 from cn

RIB 10
(mult 8 + 2 sts)

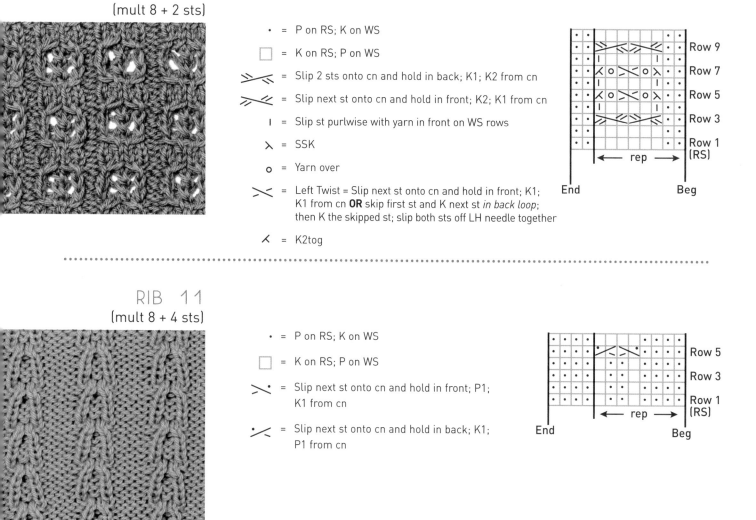

•	= P on RS; K on WS
□	= K on RS; P on WS
⤺	= Slip 2 sts onto cn and hold in back; K1; K2 from cn
⤻	= Slip next st onto cn and hold in front; K2; K1 from cn
I	= Slip st purlwise with yarn in front on WS rows
⋋	= SSK
o	= Yarn over
⤬	= Left Twist = Slip next st onto cn and hold in front; K1; K1 from cn **OR** skip first st and K next st *in back loop*; then K the skipped st; slip both sts off LH needle together
⋌	= K2tog

Row 9
Row 7
Row 5
Row 3
Row 1
(RS)

← rep →

End   Beg

RIB 11
(mult 8 + 4 sts)

•	= P on RS; K on WS
□	= K on RS; P on WS
⤬•	= Slip next st onto cn and hold in front; P1; K1 from cn
•⤬	= Slip next st onto cn and hold in back; K1; P1 from cn

Row 5
Row 3
Row 1
(RS)

← rep →

End   Beg

RIB 12
(mult 9 + 3 sts)

□	= K on RS; P on WS
•	= P on RS; K on WS
⤬	= Left Twist = Slip next st onto cn and hold in front; K1; K1 from cn **OR** skip first st and K next st *in back loop*; then K the skipped st; slip both sts off LH needle together

Row 1
(RS)

← rep →

End   Beg

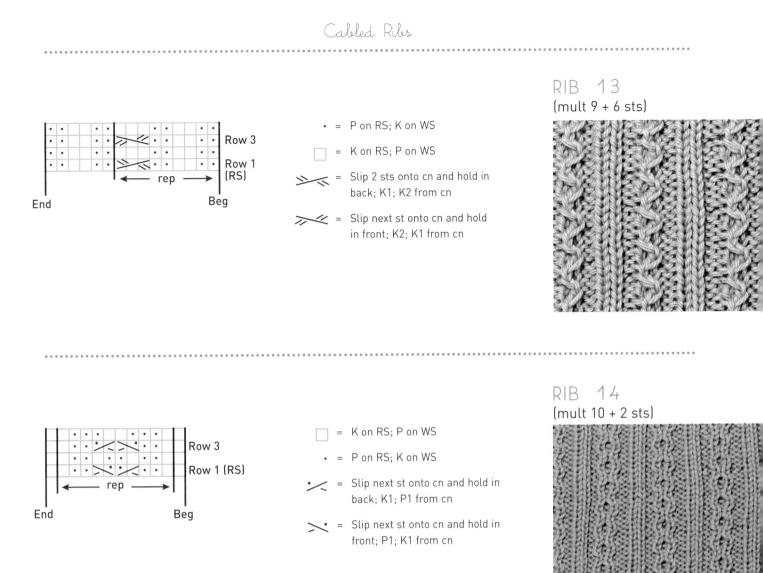

RIB 13
(mult 9 + 6 sts)

• = P on RS; K on WS

☐ = K on RS; P on WS

⧄ = Slip 2 sts onto cn and hold in back; K1; K2 from cn

⧄ = Slip next st onto cn and hold in front; K2; K1 from cn

Row 3
Row 1 (RS)
← rep →
End   Beg

RIB 14
(mult 10 + 2 sts)

☐ = K on RS; P on WS

• = P on RS; K on WS

⧄ = Slip next st onto cn and hold in back; K1; P1 from cn

⧄• = Slip next st onto cn and hold in front; P1; K1 from cn

Row 3
Row 1 (RS)
← rep →
End   Beg

RIB 15
(mult of 10 + 2 sts)

☐ = K on RS; P on WS

• = P on RS; K on WS

⧄ = Slip next st onto cn and hold in front; K next st *through back loop*; K st from cn *through back loop*

Ω = K *through back loop* on RS; P *through back loop* on WS

⧄ = Slip next st onto cn and hold in back; K next st *through back loop*; P1 from cn

⧄• = Slip next st onto cn and hold in front; P1; K1 from cn *through back loop*

Row 7
Row 5
Row 3
Row 1 (RS)
← rep →
End   Beg

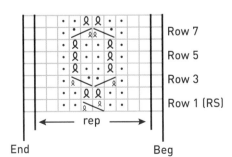

RIB 16
(mult 10 + 3 sts)

□ = K on RS; P on WS

⟩⟨• = Slip next st onto cn and hold in front; P1; K1 from cn

• = P on RS; K on WS

•⟩⟨ = Slip next st onto cn and hold in back; K1; P1 from cn

Row 11
Row 9
Row 7
Row 5
Row 3
Row 1 (RS)

← rep →

End   Beg

RIB 17
(mult 10 + 6 sts)

• = P on RS; K on WS

□ = K on RS; P on WS

⟩⟩⟨ = Slip 2 sts onto cn and hold in front; K2; K2 from cn

Row 3
Row 1 (RS)

← rep →

End   Beg

RIB 18
(mult 10 + 6 sts)

• = P on RS; K on WS

Ω = K through back loop on RS; P through back loop on WS

□ = K on RS; P on WS

⟩⟩⟨ = Slip 2 sts onto cn and hold in front; K2; K2 sts from cn

Ω⟩⟨• = Slip next st onto cn and hold in front; P1; K1 from cn through back loop

•⟩⟨Ω = Slip next st onto cn and hold in back; K next st through back loop; P1 from cn

Ω⟩⟨Ω = Slip next st onto cn and hold in front; K next st through back loop; K st from cn through back loop

Row 11
Row 9
Row 7
Row 5
Row 3
Row 1 (RS)

← rep →

End   Beg

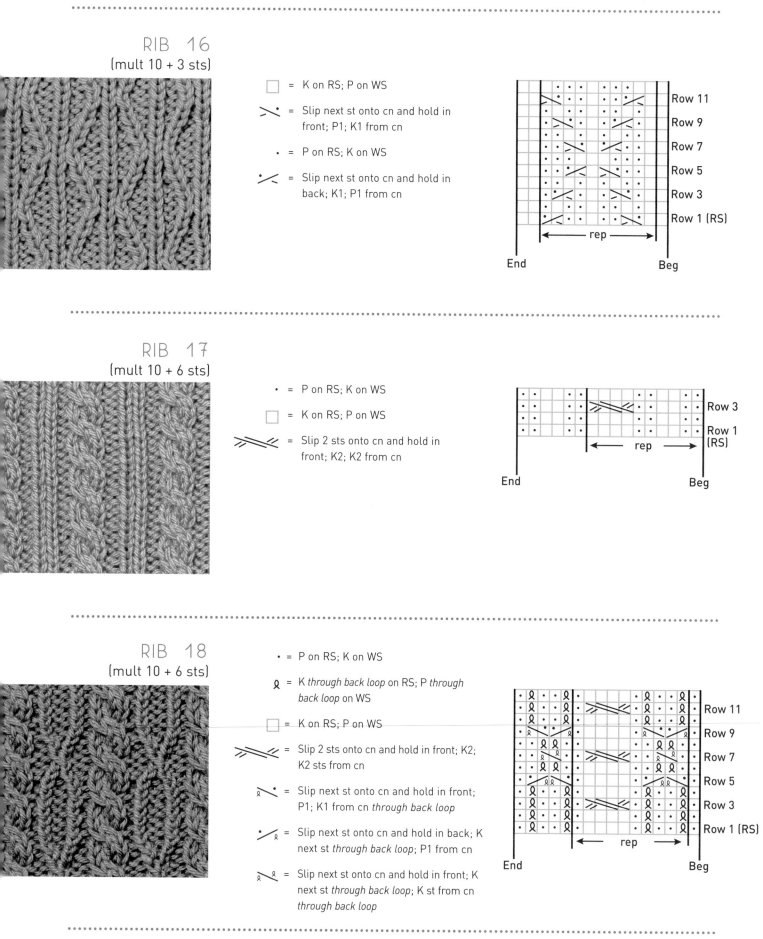

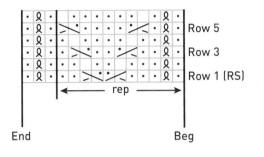

Row 5

Row 3

Row 1 (RS)

← rep →

End

Beg

- = P on RS; K on WS

ℓ = K *through back loop* on RS; P *through back loop* on WS

⟋ = Slip next st onto cn and hold in back; K1; P1 from cn

⟍ = Slip next st onto cn and hold in front; P1; K1 from cn

☐ = K on RS; P on WS

RIB 19
(mult 11 + 3 sts)

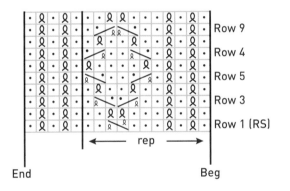

Row 9

Row 4

Row 5

Row 3

Row 1 (RS)

← rep →

End

Beg

- = P on RS; K on WS

ℓ = K *through back loop* on RS; P *through back* loop on WS

⟋ = Slip next st onto cn and hold in front; K next st *through back loop*; K st from cn *through back loop*

⟋ = Slip next st onto cn and hold in back; K next st *through back loop*; P1 from cn

⟍ = Slip next st onto cn and hold in front; P1; K1 from cn *through back loop*

RIB 20
(mult 11 + 5 sts)

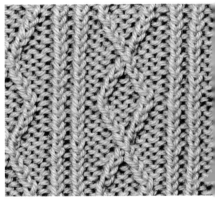

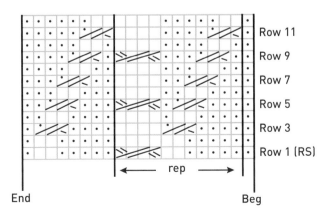

Row 11

Row 9

Row 7

Row 5

Row 3

Row 1 (RS)

← rep →

End

Beg

- = P on RS; K on WS

☐ = K on RS; P on WS

⟹ = Slip 2 sts onto cn and hold in back; K2; K2 from cn

⟋ = Slip next st onto cn and hold in back; K2; P1 from cn

RIB 21
(mult 11 + 9 sts)

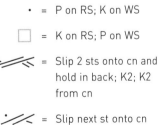

RIB 22
(mult 12 + 3 sts)

☐ = K on RS; P on WS

• = P on RS; K on WS

= Slip next st onto cn and hold in back; K next st *through back loop*; P1 from cn

ℓ = K *through back loop* on RS; P *through back loop* on WS

= Slip next st onto cn and hold in front; P1; K1 from cn *through back loop*

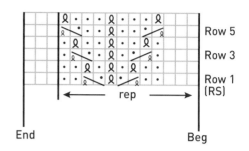

Row 5

Row 3

Row 1 (RS)

rep

End   Beg

RIB 23
(mult 14 + 5 sts)

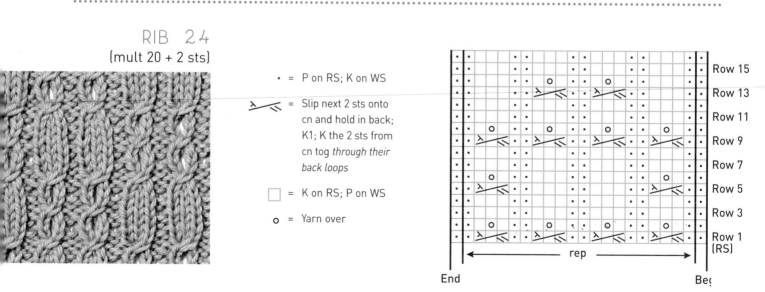

• = P on RS; K on WS

= Slip next st onto cn and hold in front; K2; K1 from cn

= Slip next st onto cn and hold in front; P1; K1 from cn

= Slip next st onto cn and hold in back; K1; P1 from cn

☐ = K on RS; P on WS

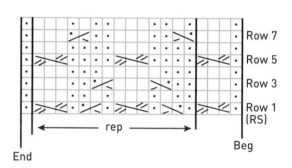

Row 7

Row 5

Row 3

Row 1 (RS)

rep

End   Beg

RIB 24
(mult 20 + 2 sts)

• = P on RS; K on WS

= Slip next 2 sts onto cn and hold in back; K1; K the 2 sts from cn tog *through their back loops*

☐ = K on RS; P on WS

o = Yarn over

Row 15
Row 13
Row 11
Row 9
Row 7
Row 5
Row 3
Row 1 (RS)

rep

End   Beg

Cabled Panels

PANEL 1
(4-st panel)

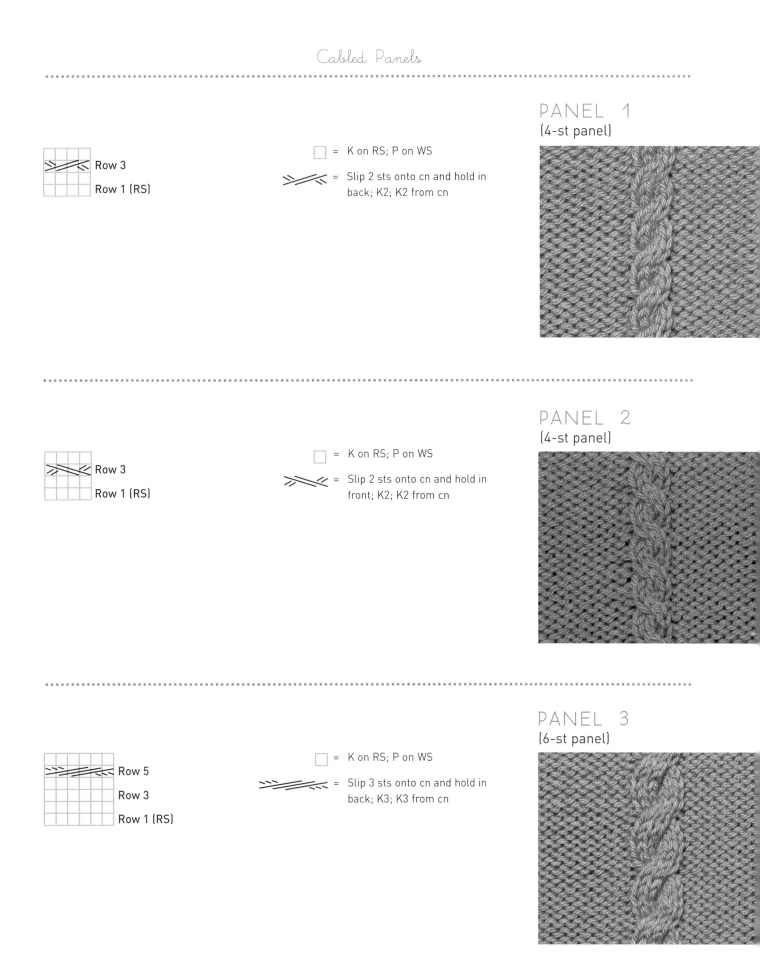

Row 3

Row 1 (RS)

☐ = K on RS; P on WS

= Slip 2 sts onto cn and hold in back; K2; K2 from cn

PANEL 2
(4-st panel)

Row 3

Row 1 (RS)

☐ = K on RS; P on WS

= Slip 2 sts onto cn and hold in front; K2; K2 from cn

PANEL 3
(6-st panel)

Row 5

Row 3

Row 1 (RS)

☐ = K on RS; P on WS

= Slip 3 sts onto cn and hold in back; K3; K3 from cn

LEFT: Cable Panel patterns (clockwise from top left): 48, 37, 39, 50, 41, 40, 30, and 42

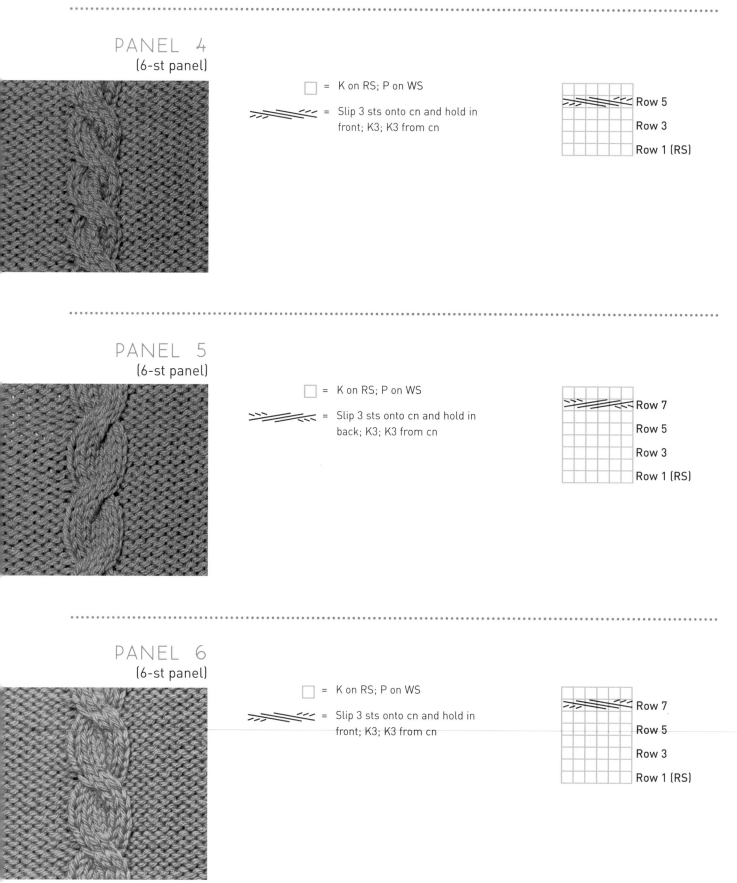

PANEL 4
(6-st panel)

☐ = K on RS; P on WS

⟩⟩⟩⟨⟨⟨ = Slip 3 sts onto cn and hold in front; K3; K3 from cn

Row 5
Row 3
Row 1 (RS)

PANEL 5
(6-st panel)

☐ = K on RS; P on WS

⟩⟩⟩⟨⟨⟨ = Slip 3 sts onto cn and hold in back; K3; K3 from cn

Row 7
Row 5
Row 3
Row 1 (RS)

PANEL 6
(6-st panel)

☐ = K on RS; P on WS

⟩⟩⟩⟨⟨⟨ = Slip 3 sts onto cn and hold in front; K3; K3 from cn

Row 7
Row 5
Row 3
Row 1 (RS)

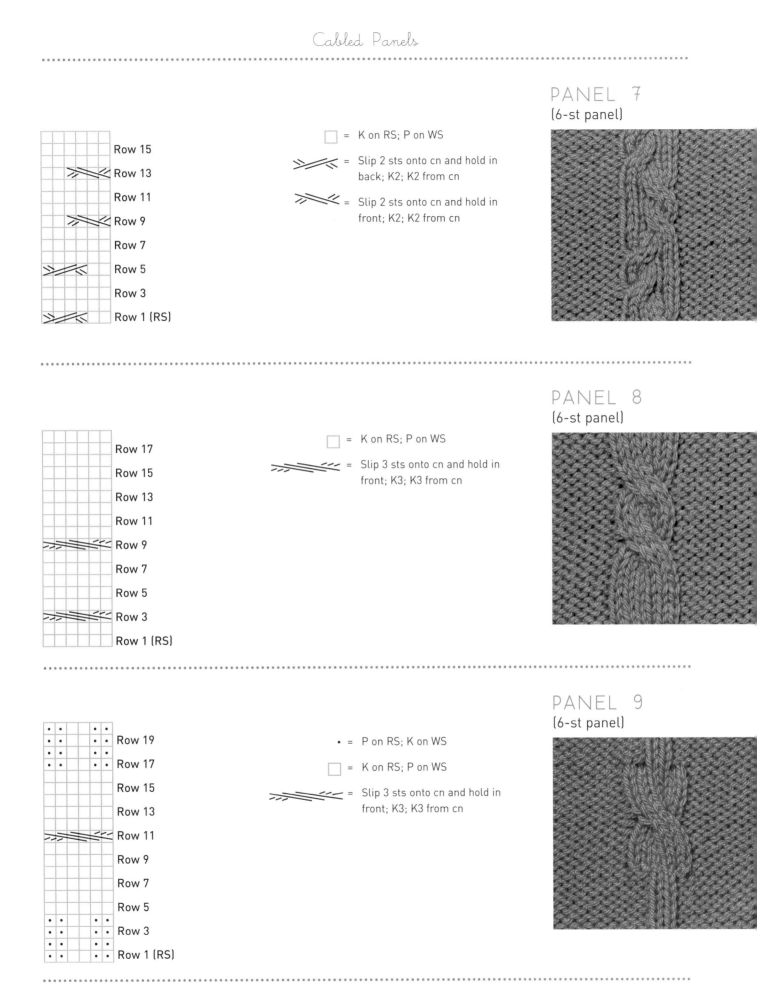

PANEL 7
(6-st panel)

Row 15
Row 13
Row 11
Row 9
Row 7
Row 5
Row 3
Row 1 (RS)

☐ = K on RS; P on WS

= Slip 2 sts onto cn and hold in back; K2; K2 from cn

= Slip 2 sts onto cn and hold in front; K2; K2 from cn

PANEL 8
(6-st panel)

Row 17
Row 15
Row 13
Row 11
Row 9
Row 7
Row 5
Row 3
Row 1 (RS)

☐ = K on RS; P on WS

= Slip 3 sts onto cn and hold in front; K3; K3 from cn

PANEL 9
(6-st panel)

Row 19
Row 17
Row 15
Row 13
Row 11
Row 9
Row 7
Row 5
Row 3
Row 1 (RS)

• = P on RS; K on WS

☐ = K on RS; P on WS

= Slip 3 sts onto cn and hold in front; K3; K3 from cn

PANEL 10
(8-st panel)

□ = K on RS; P on WS

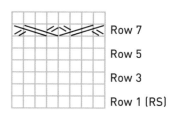

= Slip 2 sts onto cn and hold in back; K2; K2 from cn

= Slip 2 sts onto cn and hold in front; K2; K2 from cn

Row 7
Row 5
Row 3
Row 1 (RS)

PANEL 11
(8-st panel)

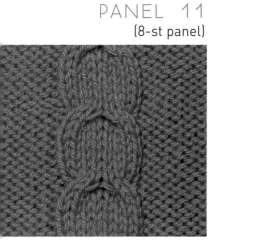

□ = K on RS; P on WS

= Slip 2 sts onto cn and hold in front; K2; K2 from cn

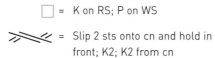

= Slip 2 sts onto cn and hold in back; K2; K2 from cn

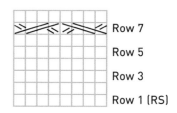

Row 7
Row 5
Row 3
Row 1 (RS)

PANEL 12
(8-st panel)

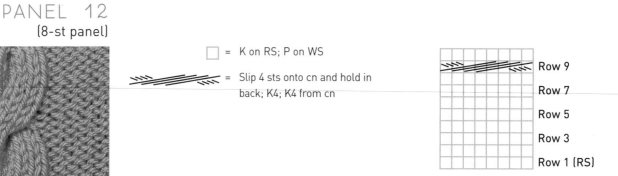

□ = K on RS; P on WS

= Slip 4 sts onto cn and hold in back; K4; K4 from cn

Row 9
Row 7
Row 5
Row 3
Row 1 (RS)

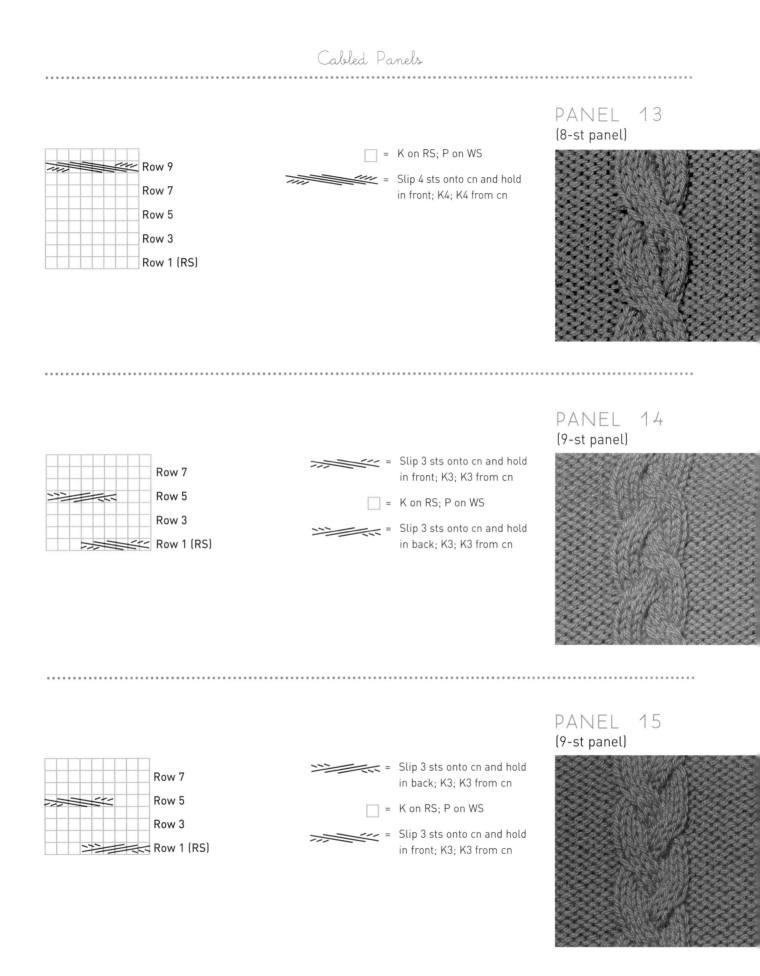

PANEL 13
(8-st panel)

Row 9
Row 7
Row 5
Row 3
Row 1 (RS)

☐ = K on RS; P on WS

= Slip 4 sts onto cn and hold in front; K4; K4 from cn

PANEL 14
(9-st panel)

Row 7
Row 5
Row 3
Row 1 (RS)

= Slip 3 sts onto cn and hold in front; K3; K3 from cn

☐ = K on RS; P on WS

= Slip 3 sts onto cn and hold in back; K3; K3 from cn

PANEL 15
(9-st panel)

Row 7
Row 5
Row 3
Row 1 (RS)

= Slip 3 sts onto cn and hold in back; K3; K3 from cn

☐ = K on RS; P on WS

= Slip 3 sts onto cn and hold in front; K3; K3 from cn

PANEL 16
(9-st panel)

= Slip 2 sts onto cn and hold in front; P1; K2 from cn

= Slip next st onto cn and hold in back; K2; P1 from cn

• = P on RS; K on WS

☐ = K on RS; P on WS

= Slip 2 sts onto cn and hold in front; K2; K2 from cn

= Slip 2 sts onto cn and hold in back; K2; K2 from cn

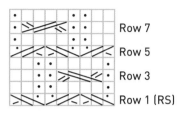

Row 7
Row 5
Row 3
Row 1 (RS)

PANEL 17
(9-st panel)

= Slip 2 sts onto cn and hold in back; K2; K2 from cn

☐ = K on RS; P on WS

= Slip 2 sts onto cn and hold in front; K2; K2 from cn

B = Bobble = K into (front, back, front) of next st, turn; P1, (P1, yarn over, P1) all into next st, P1, turn; K5, turn; P2tog, P1, P2tog, turn; slip 2 sts at once knitwise, K1, p2sso

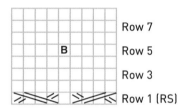

Row 7
Row 5
Row 3
Row 1 (RS)

PANEL 18
(9-st panel)

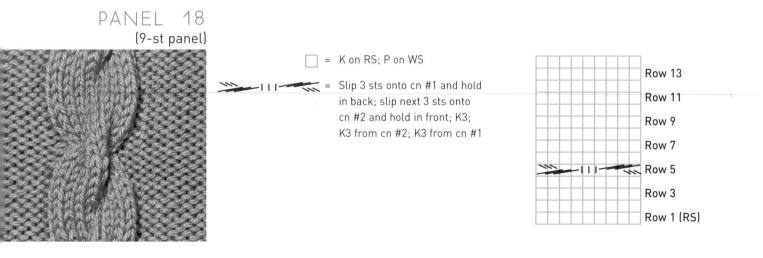

☐ = K on RS; P on WS

= Slip 3 sts onto cn #1 and hold in back; slip next 3 sts onto cn #2 and hold in front; K3; K3 from cn #2; K3 from cn #1

Row 13
Row 11
Row 9
Row 7
Row 5
Row 3
Row 1 (RS)

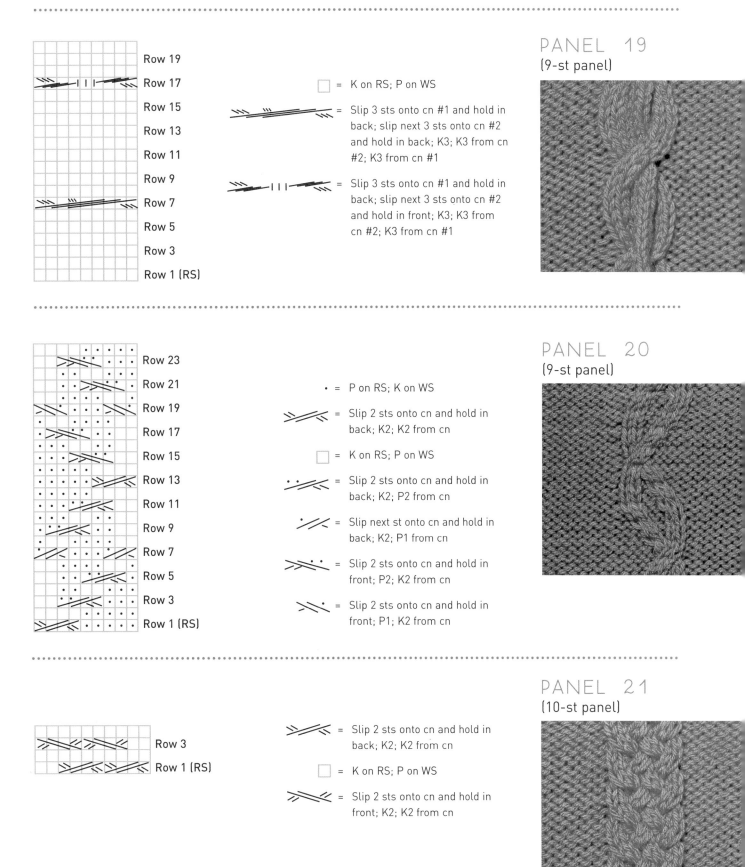

PANEL 19
(9-st panel)

□ = K on RS; P on WS

= Slip 3 sts onto cn #1 and hold in back; slip next 3 sts onto cn #2 and hold in back; K3; K3 from cn #2; K3 from cn #1

= Slip 3 sts onto cn #1 and hold in back; slip next 3 sts onto cn #2 and hold in front; K3; K3 from cn #2; K3 from cn #1

Row 19
Row 17
Row 15
Row 13
Row 11
Row 9
Row 7
Row 5
Row 3
Row 1 (RS)

PANEL 20
(9-st panel)

• = P on RS; K on WS

= Slip 2 sts onto cn and hold in back; K2; K2 from cn

□ = K on RS; P on WS

= Slip 2 sts onto cn and hold in back; K2; P2 from cn

= Slip next st onto cn and hold in back; K2; P1 from cn

= Slip 2 sts onto cn and hold in front; P2; K2 from cn

= Slip 2 sts onto cn and hold in front; P1; K2 from cn

Row 23
Row 21
Row 19
Row 17
Row 15
Row 13
Row 11
Row 9
Row 7
Row 5
Row 3
Row 1 (RS)

PANEL 21
(10-st panel)

= Slip 2 sts onto cn and hold in back; K2; K2 from cn

□ = K on RS; P on WS

= Slip 2 sts onto cn and hold in front; K2; K2 from cn

Row 3
Row 1 (RS)

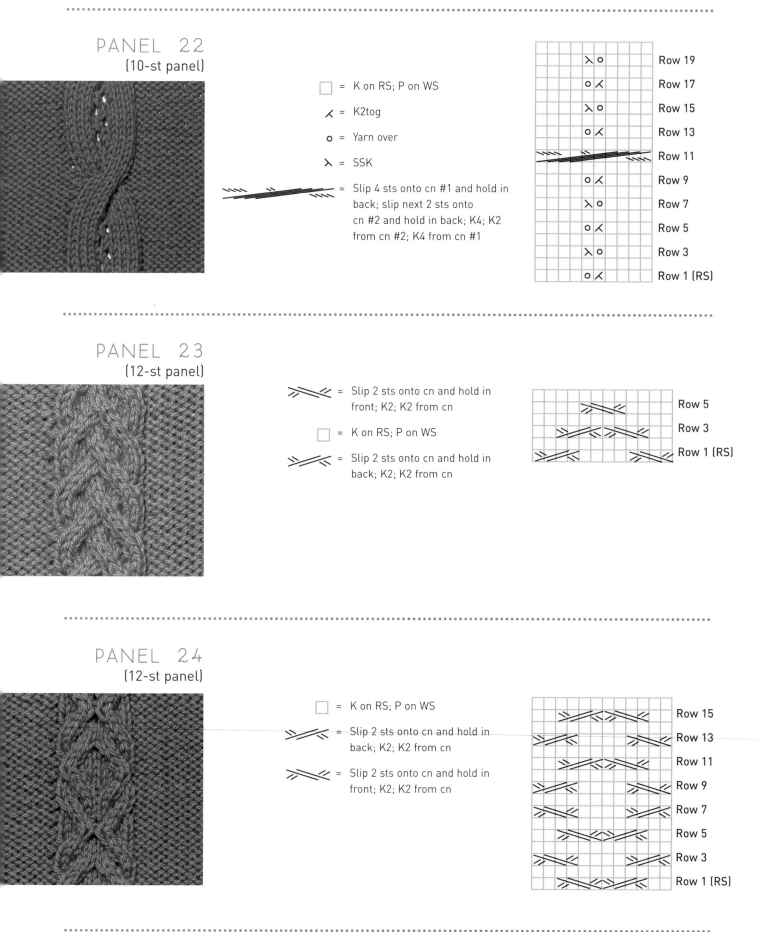

PANEL 22
(10-st panel)

☐ = K on RS; P on WS

↗ = K2tog

o = Yarn over

↘ = SSK

= Slip 4 sts onto cn #1 and hold in back; slip next 2 sts onto cn #2 and hold in back; K4; K2 from cn #2; K4 from cn #1

Row 19
Row 17
Row 15
Row 13
Row 11
Row 9
Row 7
Row 5
Row 3
Row 1 (RS)

PANEL 23
(12-st panel)

= Slip 2 sts onto cn and hold in front; K2; K2 from cn

☐ = K on RS; P on WS

= Slip 2 sts onto cn and hold in back; K2; K2 from cn

Row 5
Row 3
Row 1 (RS)

PANEL 24
(12-st panel)

☐ = K on RS; P on WS

= Slip 2 sts onto cn and hold in back; K2; K2 from cn

= Slip 2 sts onto cn and hold in front; K2; K2 from cn

Row 15
Row 13
Row 11
Row 9
Row 7
Row 5
Row 3
Row 1 (RS)

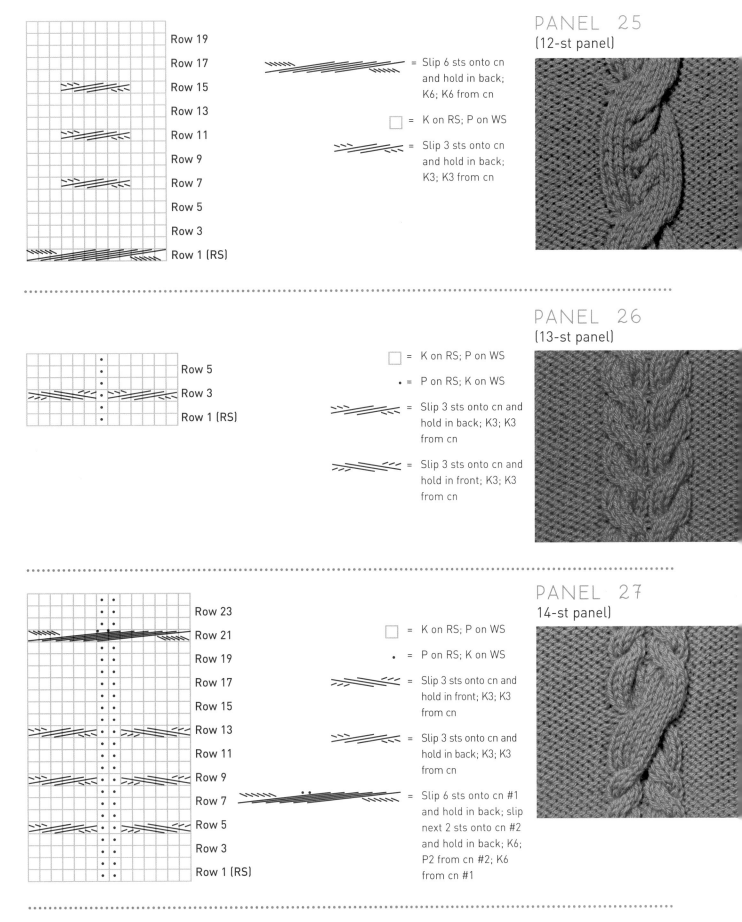

PANEL 25
(12-st panel)

Row 19
Row 17
Row 15
Row 13
Row 11
Row 9
Row 7
Row 5
Row 3
Row 1 (RS)

= Slip 6 sts onto cn and hold in back; K6; K6 from cn

☐ = K on RS; P on WS

= Slip 3 sts onto cn and hold in back; K3; K3 from cn

PANEL 26
(13-st panel)

Row 5
Row 3
Row 1 (RS)

☐ = K on RS; P on WS

• = P on RS; K on WS

= Slip 3 sts onto cn and hold in back; K3; K3 from cn

= Slip 3 sts onto cn and hold in front; K3; K3 from cn

PANEL 27
14-st panel)

Row 23
Row 21
Row 19
Row 17
Row 15
Row 13
Row 11
Row 9
Row 7
Row 5
Row 3
Row 1 (RS)

☐ = K on RS; P on WS

• = P on RS; K on WS

= Slip 3 sts onto cn and hold in front; K3; K3 from cn

= Slip 3 sts onto cn and hold in back; K3; K3 from cn

= Slip 6 sts onto cn #1 and hold in back; slip next 2 sts onto cn #2 and hold in back; K6; P2 from cn #2; K6 from cn #1

PANEL 28
(14-st panel)

• = P on RS; K on WS

$\diagdown\diagdown$ = Slip 2 sts onto cn and hold in back; K2; K2 from cn

☐ = K on RS; P on WS

$\diagdown$ = Slip next st onto cn and hold in back; K2; K1 from cn

$\diagup$ = Slip 2 sts onto cn and hold in front; K1; K2 from cn

$\diagup$ = Slip next st onto cn and hold in back; K2; P1 from cn

$\diagdown$ = Slip 2 sts onto cn and hold in front; P1; K2 from cn

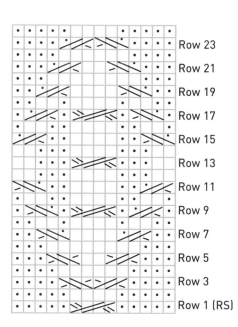

Row 23
Row 21
Row 19
Row 17
Row 15
Row 13
Row 11
Row 9
Row 7
Row 5
Row 3
Row 1 (RS)

PANEL 29
(15-st panel, inc to 21 sts)

☐ = K on RS; P on WS

• = P on RS; K on WS

▨ = No stitch

M = M1 = Insert LH needle under the horizontal strand between two sts from front to back and K it *through back loop*

⋎ = Central Double Increase = (Increases from 1 st to 3 sts) = K into back and then into front of indicated st and slip them off LH needle onto RH needle; insert point of LH needle behind the vertical strand that runs downward between the two sts just made and K *into the front* of it

⋎ = (Increases from 1 st to 3 sts) = (P, yarn over, P) into next st

$\diagup$ = Slip 3 sts onto cn and hold in front; P2; K3 from cn

$\diagdown$ = Slip 2 sts onto cn and hold in back; K3; P2 from cn

⑧ = P *through back loop*

$\diagdown\diagdown$ = Slip 3 sts onto cn and hold in back; K3; K3 from cn

$\diagdown$ = Slip 3 sts onto cn #1 and hold in front; slip next st onto cn #2 and hold in back; K3; P1 from cn #2; K3 from cn #1

⋏ = (Decreases from 7 sts to 1 st) = Slip next 4 sts with yarn in back, drop yarn; *pass the second st on RH needle over the first st on RH needle; slip first st from RH needle back to LH needle; pass the second st on LH needle over the first st on LH needle; **slip first st from LH needle back to RH needle and repeat from * to ** twice more; pick up yarn and K remaining st

chart shown on next page

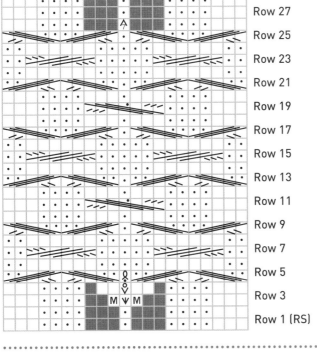

Row 27
Row 25
Row 23
Row 21
Row 19
Row 17
Row 15
Row 13
Row 11
Row 9
Row 7
Row 5
Row 3
Row 1 (RS)

PANEL 29
chart continued from previous page

Row 11
Row 9
Row 7
Row 5
Row 3
Row 1 (RS)

☐ = K on RS; P on WS

• = P on RS; K on WS

= Slip 4 sts onto cn and hold in front; K4; K4 from cn

= Slip 4 sts onto cn and hold in back; K4; K4 from cn

PANEL 30
(16-st panel)

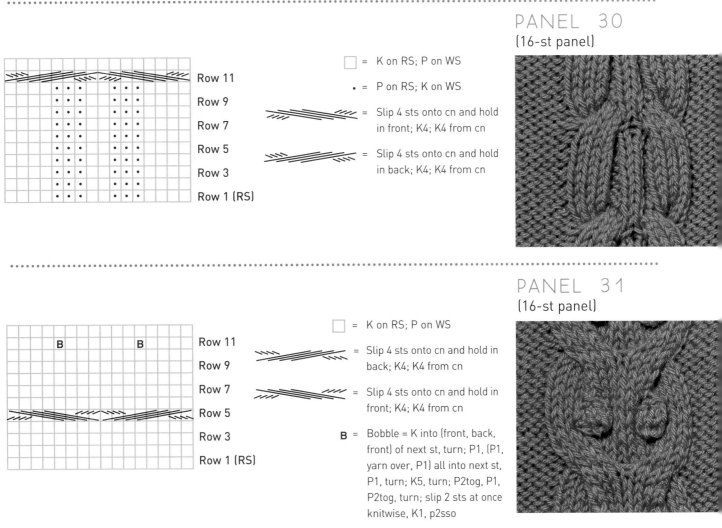

Row 11
Row 9
Row 7
Row 5
Row 3
Row 1 (RS)

☐ = K on RS; P on WS

= Slip 4 sts onto cn and hold in back; K4; K4 from cn

= Slip 4 sts onto cn and hold in front; K4; K4 from cn

B = Bobble = K into (front, back, front) of next st, turn; P1, (P1, yarn over, P1) all into next st, P1, turn; K5, turn; P2tog, P1, P2tog, turn; slip 2 sts at once knitwise, K1, p2sso

PANEL 31
(16-st panel)

PANEL 32
(16-st panel)

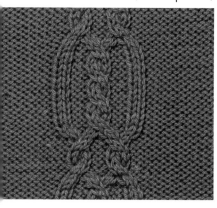

☐ = K on RS; P on WS

• = P on RS; K on WS

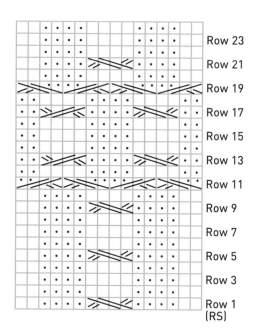 = Slip 2 sts onto cn and hold in front; K2; K2 from cn

= Slip 2 sts onto cn and hold in front; P2; K2 from cn

= Slip 2 sts onto cn and hold in back; K2; P2 from cn

= Slip 2 sts onto cn and hold in back; K2; K2 from cn

Row 23
Row 21
Row 19
Row 17
Row 15
Row 13
Row 11
Row 9
Row 7
Row 5
Row 3
Row 1 (RS)

PANEL 33
(16-st panel)

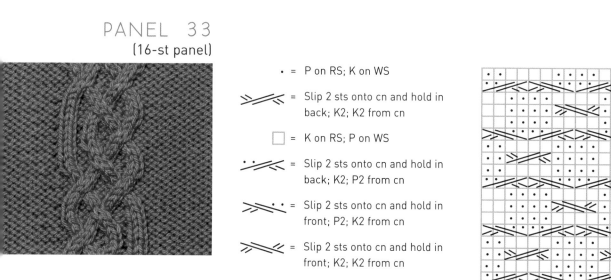

• = P on RS; K on WS

= Slip 2 sts onto cn and hold in back; K2; K2 from cn

☐ = K on RS; P on WS

= Slip 2 sts onto cn and hold in back; K2; P2 from cn

= Slip 2 sts onto cn and hold in front; P2; K2 from cn

= Slip 2 sts onto cn and hold in front; K2; K2 from cn

Row 31
Row 29
Row 27
Row 25
Row 23
Row 21
Row 19
Row 17
Row 15
Row 13
Row 11
Row 9
Row 7
Row 5
Row 3
Row 1 (RS)

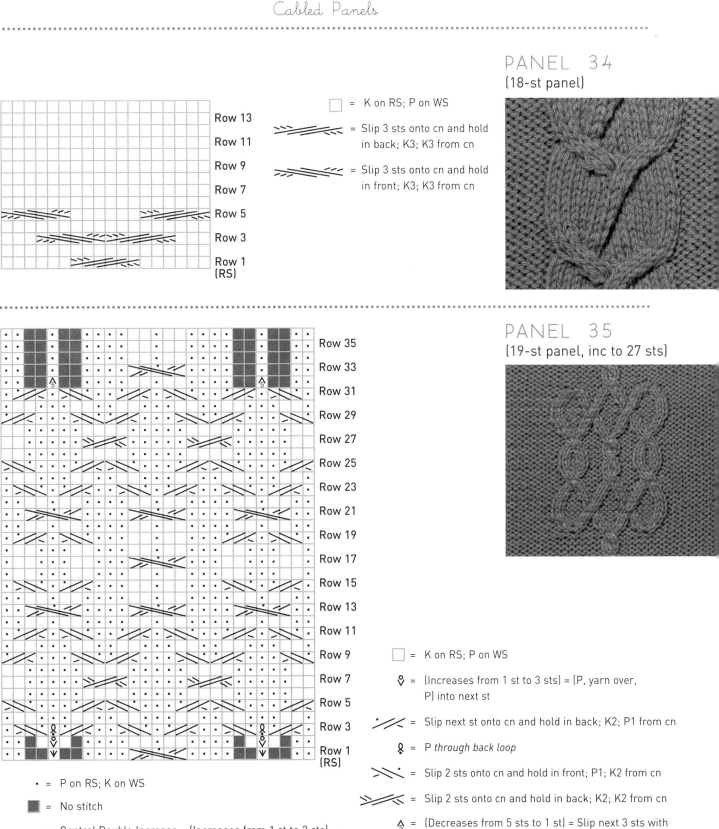

Row 13
Row 11
Row 9
Row 7
Row 5
Row 3
Row 1
(RS)

☐ = K on RS; P on WS

= Slip 3 sts onto cn and hold in back; K3; K3 from cn

= Slip 3 sts onto cn and hold in front; K3; K3 from cn

Row 35
Row 33
Row 31
Row 29
Row 27
Row 25
Row 23
Row 21
Row 19
Row 17
Row 15
Row 13
Row 11
Row 9
Row 7
Row 5
Row 3
Row 1
(RS)

☐ = K on RS; P on WS

⋎ = (Increases from 1 st to 3 sts) = (P, yarn over, P) into next st

= Slip next st onto cn and hold in back; K2; P1 from cn

⋔ = P through back loop

= Slip 2 sts onto cn and hold in front; P1; K2 from cn

= Slip 2 sts onto cn and hold in back; K2; K2 from cn

⩗₅ = (Decreases from 5 sts to 1 st) = Slip next 3 sts with yarn in back, drop yarn; *pass the second st on RH needle over the first st on RH needle; slip first st from RH needle back to LH needle; pass the second st on LH needle over the first st on LH needle; **slip first st from LH needle back to RH needle and repeat from * to ** once more; pick up yarn and K remaining st

• = P on RS; K on WS

▪ = No stitch

⋎ = Central Double Increase = (Increases from 1 st to 3 sts) = K into back and then into front of indicated st and slip them off LH needle onto RH needle; insert point of LH needle behind the vertical strand that runs downward between the two sts just made and K *into the front* of it

= Slip 2 sts onto cn #1 and hold in front; slip next st onto cn #2 and hold in back; K2; P1 from cn #2; K2 from cn #1

PANEL 36
(20-st panel)

- • = P on RS; K on WS

- ⟋⟍ = Slip next st onto cn and hold in back; K1; P1 from cn

- ☐ = K on RS; P on WS

- ⟍⟋ = Slip next st onto cn and hold in front; P1; K1 from cn

- **B** = Bobble = K into (front, back, front) of next st, turn; P1, (P1, yarn over, P1) all into next st, P1, turn; K5, turn; P2tog, P1, P2tog, turn; slip 2 sts at once knitwise, K1, p2sso

- = Slip 4 sts onto cn and hold in front; K4; K4 from cn

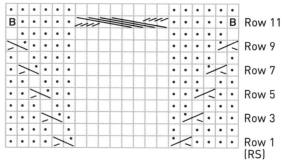

PANEL 37
(21-st panel)

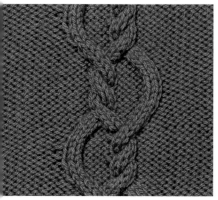

- • = P on RS; K on WS

- = Slip 3 sts onto cn and hold in back; K3; K3 from cn

- ☐ = K on RS; P on WS

- = Slip next st onto cn and hold in back; K3; P1 from cn

- = Slip 2 sts onto cn and hold in back; K3; P2 from cn

- = Slip 3 sts onto cn and hold in front; P2; K3 from cn

- = Slip 3 sts onto cn and hold in front; K3; K3 from cn

- = Slip 3 sts onto cn and hold in front; P1; K3 from cn

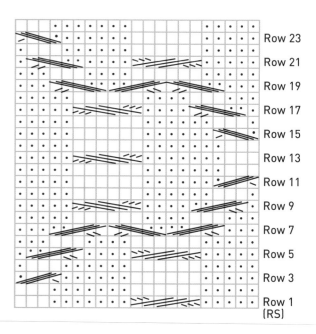

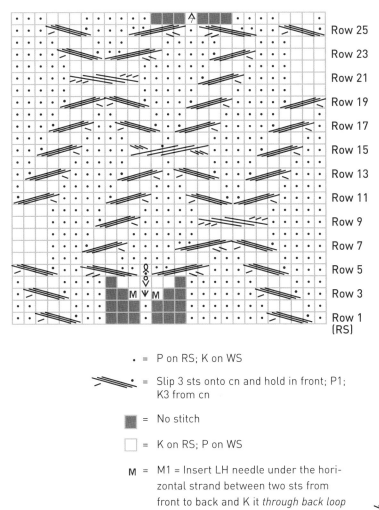

Row 25
Row 23
Row 21
Row 19
Row 17
Row 15
Row 13
Row 11
Row 9
Row 7
Row 5
Row 3
Row 1
(RS)

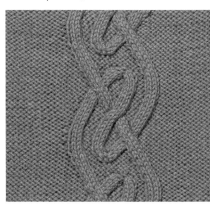

• = P on RS; K on WS

= Slip 3 sts onto cn and hold in front; P1; K3 from cn

= No stitch

= K on RS; P on WS

M = M1 = Insert LH needle under the horizontal strand between two sts from front to back and K it *through back loop*

Ψ = Central Double Increase = (Increases from 1 st to 3 sts) = K into back and then into front of indicated st and slip them off LH needle onto RH needle; insert point of LH needle behind the vertical strand that runs downward between the two sts just made and K *into the front* of it

Ϙ = (Increases from 1 st to 3 sts) = (P, yarn over, P) into next st

= Slip 2 sts onto cn and hold in back; K3; P2 from cn

Ϙ = P *through back loop*

= Slip 3 sts onto cn and hold in front; P2; K3 from cn

= Slip next st onto cn and hold in back; K3; P1 from cn

= Slip 3 sts onto cn and hold in front; K3; K3 from cn

= Slip 3 sts onto cn #1 and hold in back; slip next st onto cn #2 and hold in back; K3; P1 from cn #2; K3 from cn #1

Λ = (Decreases from 7 sts to 1 st) = Slip next 4 sts with yarn in back, drop yarn; *pass the second st on RH needle over the first st on RH needle; slip first st from RH needle back to LH needle; pass the second st on LH needle over the first st on LH needle**; slip first st from LH needle back to RH needle and repeat from * to ** twice more; pick up yarn and K remaining st

PANEL 39
(22-st panel)

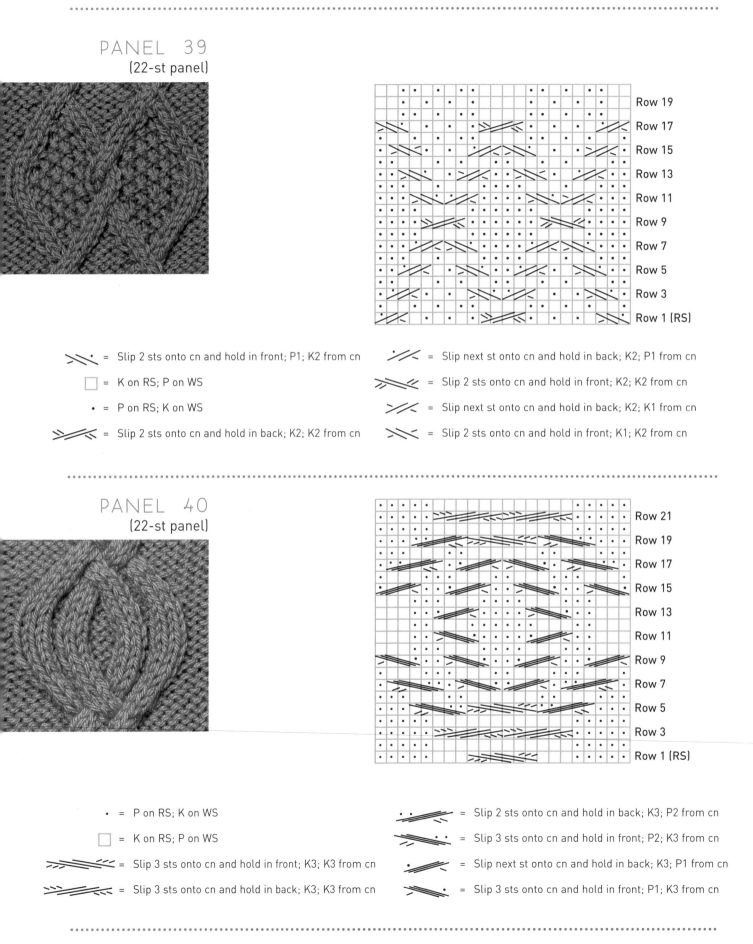

Row 19
Row 17
Row 15
Row 13
Row 11
Row 9
Row 7
Row 5
Row 3
Row 1 (RS)

= Slip 2 sts onto cn and hold in front; P1; K2 from cn

□ = K on RS; P on WS

• = P on RS; K on WS

= Slip 2 sts onto cn and hold in back; K2; K2 from cn

= Slip next st onto cn and hold in back; K2; P1 from cn

= Slip 2 sts onto cn and hold in front; K2; K2 from cn

= Slip next st onto cn and hold in back; K2; K1 from cn

= Slip 2 sts onto cn and hold in front; K1; K2 from cn

PANEL 40
(22-st panel)

Row 21
Row 19
Row 17
Row 15
Row 13
Row 11
Row 9
Row 7
Row 5
Row 3
Row 1 (RS)

• = P on RS; K on WS

□ = K on RS; P on WS

= Slip 3 sts onto cn and hold in front; K3; K3 from cn

= Slip 3 sts onto cn and hold in back; K3; K3 from cn

= Slip 2 sts onto cn and hold in back; K3; P2 from cn

= Slip 3 sts onto cn and hold in front; P2; K3 from cn

= Slip next st onto cn and hold in back; K3; P1 from cn

= Slip 3 sts onto cn and hold in front; P1; K3 from cn

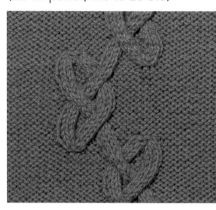

PANEL 41
(22-st panel, inc to 28 sts)

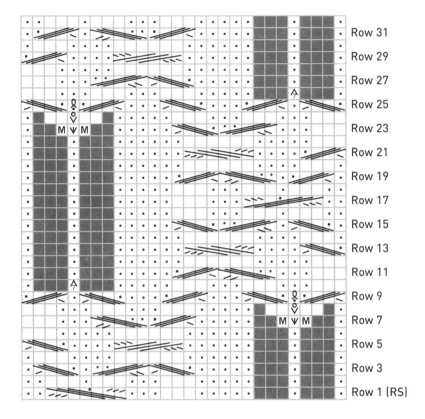

Row 31
Row 29
Row 27
Row 25
Row 23
Row 21
Row 19
Row 17
Row 15
Row 13
Row 11
Row 9
Row 7
Row 5
Row 3
Row 1 (RS)

• = P on RS; K on WS

▪ = No stitch

☐ = K on RS; P on WS

= Slip 3 sts onto cn #1 and hold in front; slip next st onto cn #2 and hold in back; K3; P1 from cn #2; K3 from cn #1

= Slip 3 sts onto cn and hold in front; P1; K3 from cn

= Slip 2 sts onto cn and hold in back; K3; P2 from cn

= Slip 3 sts onto cn and hold in back; K3; K3 from cn

M = M1 = Insert LH needle under the horizontal strand between two sts from front to back and K it *through back loop*

Ⅴ = Central Double Increase = (Increases from 1 st to 3 sts) = K into back and then into front of indicated st and slip them off LH needle onto RH needle; insert point of LH needle behind the vertical strand that runs downward between the two sts just made and K *into the front* of it

= Slip 3 sts onto cn and hold in front; P2; K3 from cn

 = (Increases from 1 st to 3 sts) = (P, yarn over, P) into next st

= Slip next st onto cn and hold in back; K3; P1 from cn

⅋ = P *through back loop*

⋏ = (Decreases from 7 sts to 1 st) = Slip next 4 sts with yarn in back, drop yarn; *pass the second st on RH needle over the first st on RH needle; slip first st from RH needle back to LH needle; pass the second st on LH needle over the first st on LH needle; **slip first st from LH needle back to RH needle and repeat from * to ** twice more; pick up yarn and K remaining st

= Slip 3 sts onto cn and hold in front; K3; K3 from cn

= Slip 3 sts onto cn #1 and hold in back; slip next st onto cn #2 and hold in back; K3; P1 from cn #2; K3 from cn #1

PANEL 42
(22-st panel, inc to 30 sts)

Row 23
Row 21
Row 19
Row 17
Row 15
Row 13
Row 11
Row 9
Row 7
Row 5
Row 3
Row 1 (RS)

• = P on RS; K on WS

▨ = No stitch

⟩⟩⟨⟨ = Slip 2 sts onto cn and hold in front; K2; K2 from cn

☐ = K on RS; P on WS

⟩⟩⟨⟨ = Slip 2 sts onto cn and hold in back; K2; P2 from cn

⟩⟩⟨⟨ = Slip 2 sts onto cn and hold in front; P2; K2 from cn

M = M1 = Insert LH needle under the horizontal strand between two sts from front to back and K it *through back loop*

V = Central Double Increase = (Increases from 1 st to 3 sts) = K into back and then into front of indicated st and slip them off LH needle onto RH needle; insert point of LH needle behind the vertical strand that runs downward between the two sts just made and K *into the front* of it

⟩⟩⟨⟨ = Slip 2 sts onto cn #1 and hold in back; slip next st onto cn #2 and hold in back; K2; P1 from cn #2; K2 from cn #1

⑸ = (Decreases from 5 sts to 1 st) = Slip next 3 sts with yarn in back, drop yarn; *pass the second st on RH needle over the first st on RH needle; slip first st from RH needle back to LH needle; pass the second st on LH needle over the first st on LH needle; **slip first st from LH needle back to RH needle and repeat from * to ** once more; pick up yarn and K remaining st

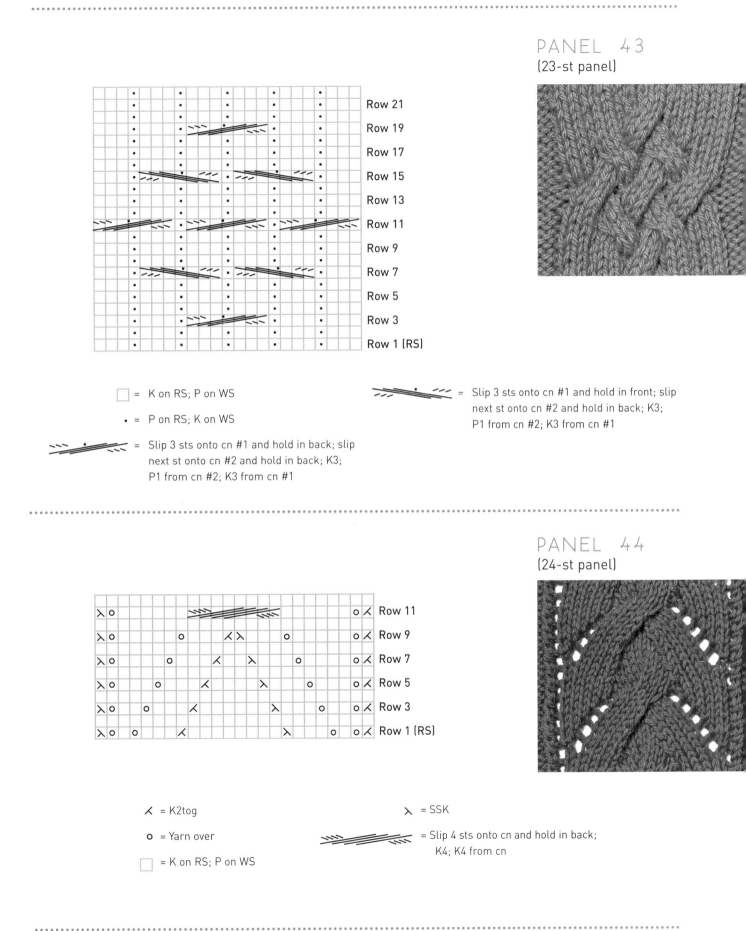

Row 21
Row 19
Row 17
Row 15
Row 13
Row 11
Row 9
Row 7
Row 5
Row 3
Row 1 (RS)

☐ = K on RS; P on WS

• = P on RS; K on WS

= Slip 3 sts onto cn #1 and hold in back; slip
next st onto cn #2 and hold in back; K3;
P1 from cn #2; K3 from cn #1

= Slip 3 sts onto cn #1 and hold in front; slip
next st onto cn #2 and hold in back; K3;
P1 from cn #2; K3 from cn #1

Row 11
Row 9
Row 7
Row 5
Row 3
Row 1 (RS)

⋏ = K2tog

o = Yarn over

☐ = K on RS; P on WS

⋋ = SSK

= Slip 4 sts onto cn and hold in back;
K4; K4 from cn

PANEL 45
(24-st panel, inc to 36 sts)

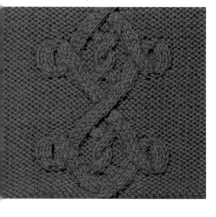

Row 19
Row 17
Row 15
Row 13
Row 11
Row 9
Row 7
Row 5
Row 3
Row 1 (RS)

• = P on RS; K on WS

■ = No stitch

= Slip 3 sts onto cn and hold in back; K3; K3 from cn

☐ = K on RS; P on WS

= Slip 2 sts onto cn and hold in back; K3; P2 from cn

= Slip 3 sts onto cn and hold in front; P2; K3 from cn

= Slip 2 sts onto cn and hold in back; K3; K2 from cn

= Slip 3 sts onto cn and hold in front; K2; K3 from cn

M = M1 = Insert LH needle under the horizontal strand between two sts from front to back and K it *through back loop*

Ⅴ = Central Double Increase = (Increases from 1 st to 3 sts) = K into back and then into front of indicated st and slip them off LH needle onto RH needle; insert point of LH needle behind the vertical strand that runs downward between the two sts just made and K *into the front* of it

= Slip next st onto cn and hold in back; K3; P1 from cn

= Slip 2 sts onto cn and hold in front; P2; K2 from cn

= Slip 2 sts onto cn and hold in back; K2; P2 from cn

= Slip 3 sts onto cn and hold in front; P1; K3 from cn

⅋ = (Increases from 1 st to 3 sts) = (P, yarn over, P) into next st

Ⴋ = P through back loop

= Slip 2 sts onto cn and hold in back; K2; K2 from cn

= Slip 3 sts onto cn and hold in front; K3; K3 from cn

Ⴕ = (Decreases from 7 sts to 1 st) = Slip next 4 sts with yarn in back, drop yarn; *pass the second st on RH needle over the first st on RH needle; slip first st from RH needle back to LH needle; pass the second st on LH needle over the first st on LH needle**; slip first st from LH needle back to RH needle and repeat from * to ** twice more; pick up yarn and K remaining st

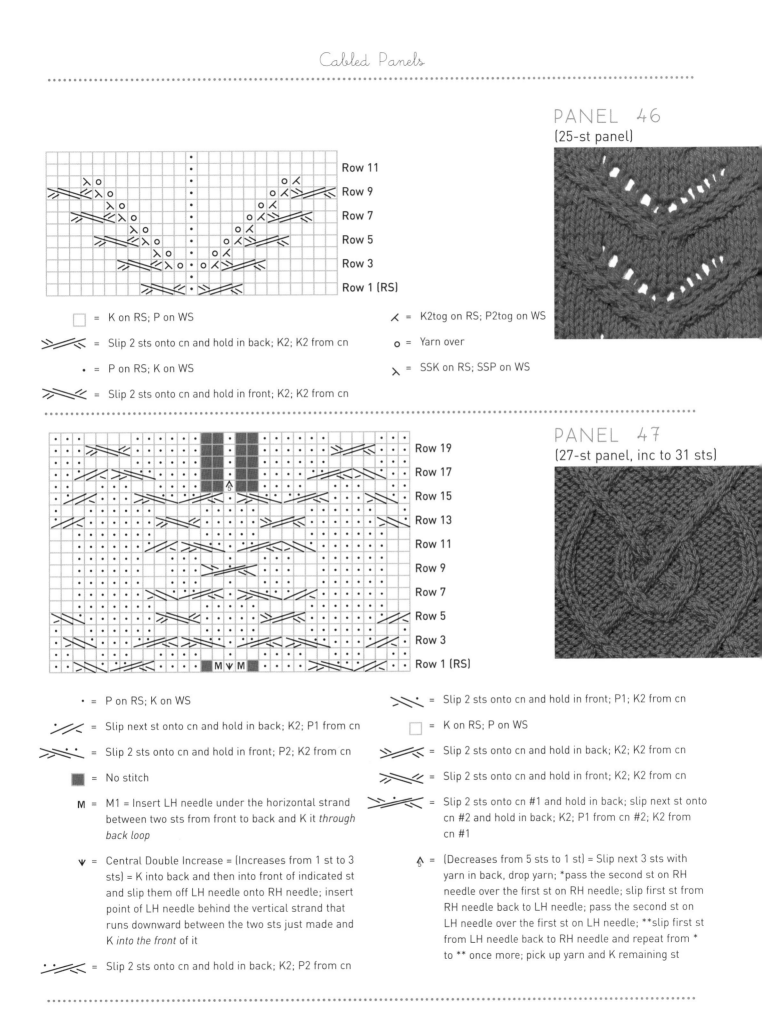

Row 11
Row 9
Row 7
Row 5
Row 3
Row 1 (RS)

☐ = K on RS; P on WS

⤢ = Slip 2 sts onto cn and hold in back; K2; K2 from cn

• = P on RS; K on WS

⤡ = Slip 2 sts onto cn and hold in front; K2; K2 from cn

⋏ = K2tog on RS; P2tog on WS

o = Yarn over

⋋ = SSK on RS; SSP on WS

Row 19
Row 17
Row 15
Row 13
Row 11
Row 9
Row 7
Row 5
Row 3
Row 1 (RS)

• = P on RS; K on WS

⋰⤢ = Slip next st onto cn and hold in back; K2; P1 from cn

⤡⋰ = Slip 2 sts onto cn and hold in front; P2; K2 from cn

▓ = No stitch

M = M1 = Insert LH needle under the horizontal strand between two sts from front to back and K it *through back loop*

⩔ = Central Double Increase = (Increases from 1 st to 3 sts) = K into back and then into front of indicated st and slip them off LH needle onto RH needle; insert point of LH needle behind the vertical strand that runs downward between the two sts just made and K *into the front* of it

⋰⤡ = Slip 2 sts onto cn and hold in back; K2; P2 from cn

⤡⋰ = Slip 2 sts onto cn and hold in front; P1; K2 from cn

☐ = K on RS; P on WS

⤢ = Slip 2 sts onto cn and hold in back; K2; K2 from cn

⤡ = Slip 2 sts onto cn and hold in front; K2; K2 from cn

⤢⋰ = Slip 2 sts onto cn #1 and hold in back; slip next st onto cn #2 and hold in back; K2; P1 from cn #2; K2 from cn #1

⩕₅ = (Decreases from 5 sts to 1 st) = Slip next 3 sts with yarn in back, drop yarn; *pass the second st on RH needle over the first st on RH needle; slip first st from RH needle back to LH needle; pass the second st on LH needle over the first st on LH needle; **slip first st from LH needle back to RH needle and repeat from * to ** once more; pick up yarn and K remaining st

PANEL 48
(27-st panel, inc to 35 sts)

Row 23
Row 21
Row 19
Row 17
Row 15
Row 13
Row 11
Row 9
Row 7
Row 5
Row 3
Row 1 (RS)

• = P on RS; K on WS

▪ = No stitch

= Slip 2 sts onto cn #1 and hold in front; slip next st onto cn #2 and hold in back; K2; P1 from cn #2; K2 from cn #1

☐ = K on RS; P on WS

= Slip 2 sts onto cn and hold in back; K2; P2 from cn

= Slip 2 sts onto cn and hold in front; P2; K2 from cn

M = M1 = Insert LH needle under the horizontal strand between two sts from front to back and K it through back loop

Ψ = Central Double Increase = (Increases from 1 st to 3 sts) = K into back and then into front of indicated st and slip them off LH needle onto RH needle; insert point of LH needle behind the vertical strand that runs downward between the two sts just made and K *into the front* of it

= Slip 2 sts onto cn and hold in back; K2; K2 from cn

Λ/5 = (Decreases from 5 sts to 1 st) = Slip next 3 sts with yarn in back, drop yarn; *pass the second st on RH needle over the first st on RH needle; slip first st from RH needle back to LH needle; pass the second st on LH needle over the first st on LH needle; **slip first st from LH needle back to RH needle and repeat from * to ** once more; pick up yarn and K remaining st

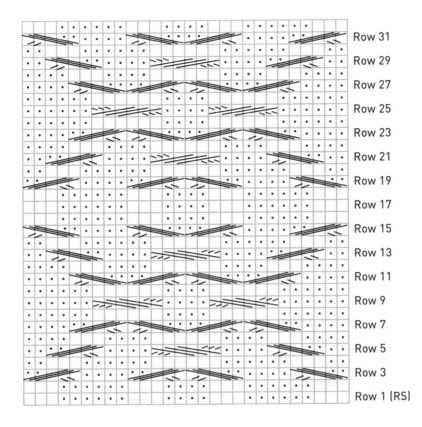

Row 31
Row 29
Row 27
Row 25
Row 23
Row 21
Row 19
Row 17
Row 15
Row 13
Row 11
Row 9
Row 7
Row 5
Row 3
Row 1 (RS)

☐ = K on RS; P on WS

• = P on RS; K on WS

= Slip 3 sts onto cn and hold in front; P2; K3 from cn

= Slip 2 sts onto cn and hold in back; K3; P2 from cn

= Slip 3 sts onto cn and hold in front; K3; K3 from cn

= Slip 3 sts onto cn and hold in back; K3; K3 from cn

PANEL 50
(28-st panel)

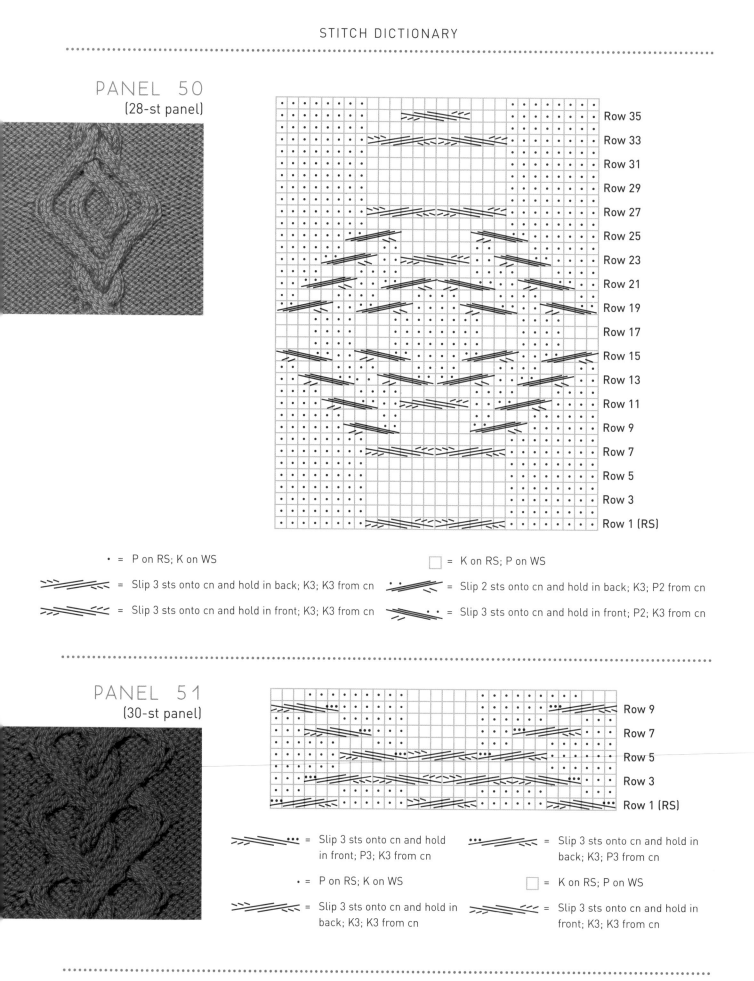

Row 35
Row 33
Row 31
Row 29
Row 27
Row 25
Row 23
Row 21
Row 19
Row 17
Row 15
Row 13
Row 11
Row 9
Row 7
Row 5
Row 3
Row 1 (RS)

• = P on RS; K on WS

☐ = K on RS; P on WS

= Slip 3 sts onto cn and hold in back; K3; K3 from cn

= Slip 2 sts onto cn and hold in back; K3; P2 from cn

= Slip 3 sts onto cn and hold in front; K3; K3 from cn

= Slip 3 sts onto cn and hold in front; P2; K3 from cn

PANEL 51
(30-st panel)

Row 9
Row 7
Row 5
Row 3
Row 1 (RS)

= Slip 3 sts onto cn and hold in front; P3; K3 from cn

= Slip 3 sts onto cn and hold in back; K3; P3 from cn

• = P on RS; K on WS

☐ = K on RS; P on WS

= Slip 3 sts onto cn and hold in back; K3; K3 from cn

= Slip 3 sts onto cn and hold in front; K3; K3 from cn

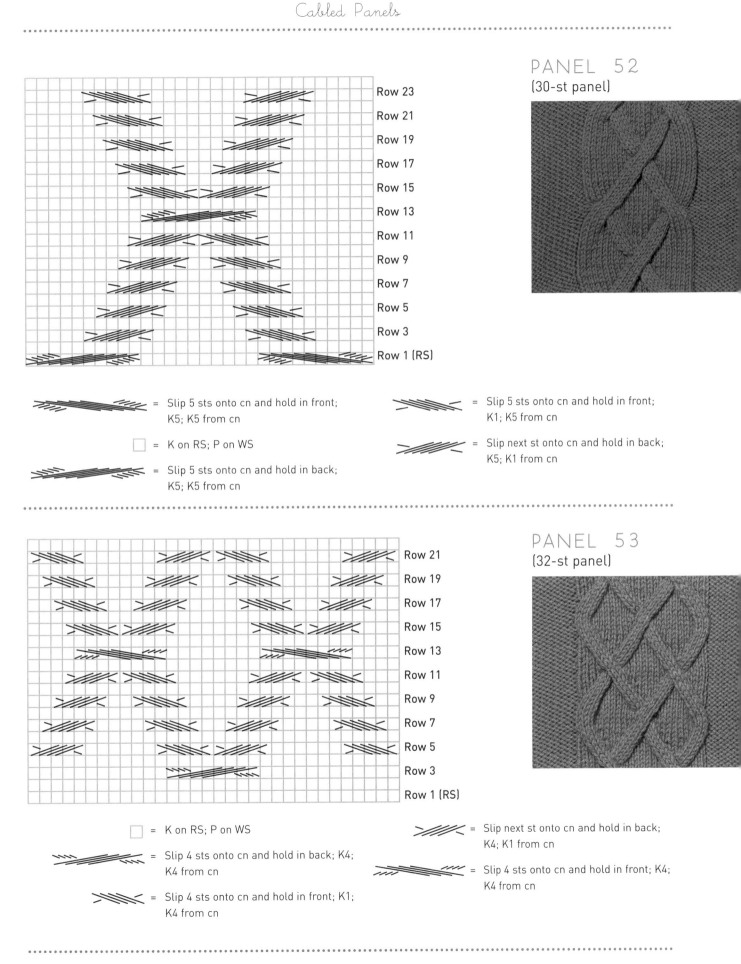

Row 23
Row 21
Row 19
Row 17
Row 15
Row 13
Row 11
Row 9
Row 7
Row 5
Row 3
Row 1 (RS)

(30-st panel)

= Slip 5 sts onto cn and hold in front; K5; K5 from cn

= K on RS; P on WS

= Slip 5 sts onto cn and hold in back; K5; K5 from cn

= Slip 5 sts onto cn and hold in front; K1; K5 from cn

= Slip next st onto cn and hold in back; K5; K1 from cn

Row 21
Row 19
Row 17
Row 15
Row 13
Row 11
Row 9
Row 7
Row 5
Row 3
Row 1 (RS)

(32-st panel)

= K on RS; P on WS

= Slip 4 sts onto cn and hold in back; K4; K4 from cn

= Slip 4 sts onto cn and hold in front; K1; K4 from cn

= Slip next st onto cn and hold in back; K4; K1 from cn

= Slip 4 sts onto cn and hold in front; K4; K4 from cn

PANEL 54
(32-st panel)

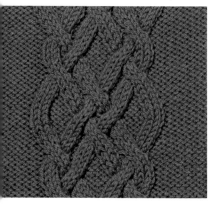

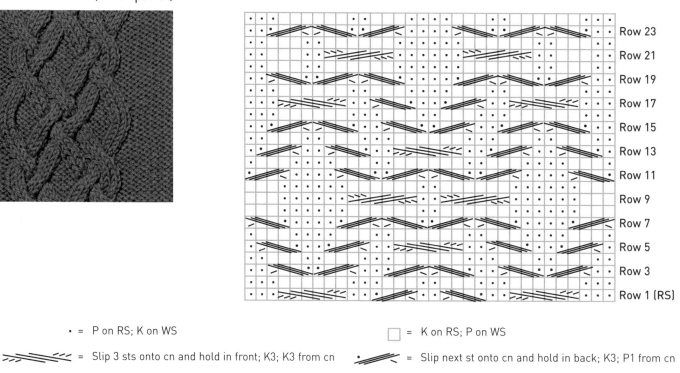

Row 23
Row 21
Row 19
Row 17
Row 15
Row 13
Row 11
Row 9
Row 7
Row 5
Row 3
Row 1 (RS)

• = P on RS; K on WS

☐ = K on RS; P on WS

= Slip 3 sts onto cn and hold in front; K3; K3 from cn

= Slip next st onto cn and hold in back; K3; P1 from cn

= Slip 3 sts onto cn and hold in front; P1; K3 from cn

= Slip 3 sts onto cn and hold in back; K3; K3 from cn

Allover Patterns

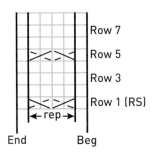

End · Beg

□ = K on RS; P on WS

>< = Right Twist = Slip next st onto cn and hold in back; K1; K1 from cn **OR** K2tog, leaving them on LH needle; insert point of RH needle between these 2 sts and K the first one again

>< = Left Twist = Slip next st onto cn and hold in front; K1; K1 from cn **OR** skip first st and K next st *in back loop*; then K the skipped st; slip both sts off LH needle together

ALLOVER 1
(mult 4 + 2 sts)

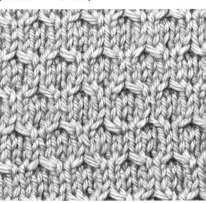

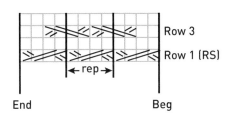

End · Beg

>= = Slip 2 sts onto cn and hold in back; K2; K2 from cn

□ = K on RS; P on WS

>= = Slip 2 sts onto cn and hold in front; K2; K2 from cn

ALLOVER 2
(mult 4 + 9 sts)

LEFT: Allover patterns (clockwise from top left): 37, 31, 43, 41, 38, 4, 3, and 39

ALLOVER 3
(mult 6 + 2 sts)

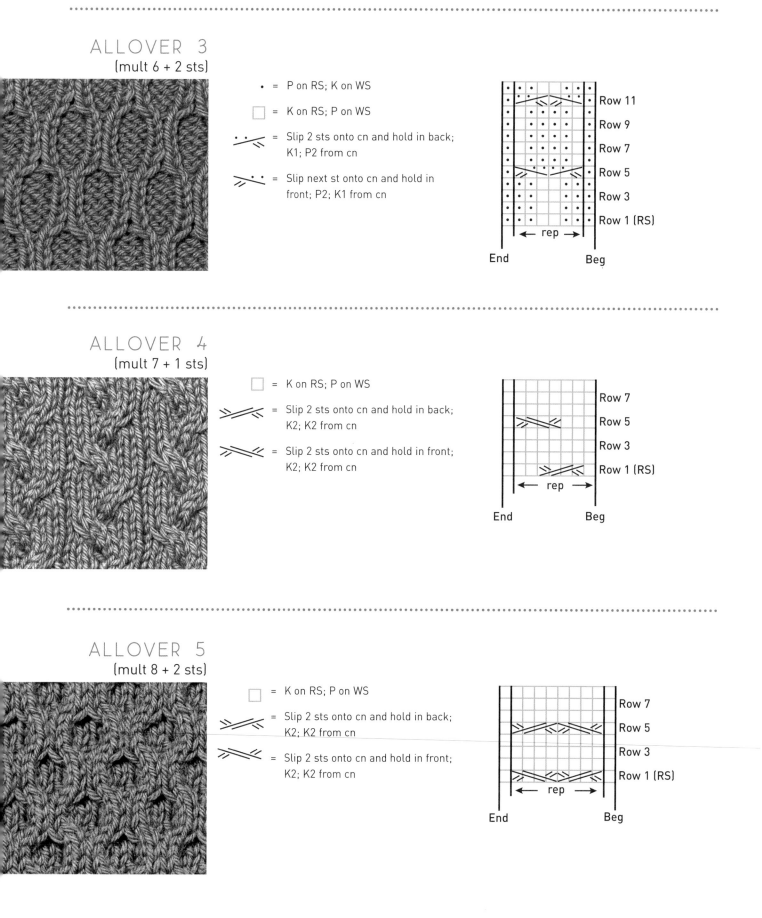

• = P on RS; K on WS

☐ = K on RS; P on WS

= Slip 2 sts onto cn and hold in back; K1; P2 from cn

= Slip next st onto cn and hold in front; P2; K1 from cn

Row 11
Row 9
Row 7
Row 5
Row 3
Row 1 (RS)

← rep →

End   Beg

ALLOVER 4
(mult 7 + 1 sts)

☐ = K on RS; P on WS

= Slip 2 sts onto cn and hold in back; K2; K2 from cn

= Slip 2 sts onto cn and hold in front; K2; K2 from cn

Row 7
Row 5
Row 3
Row 1 (RS)

← rep →

End   Beg

ALLOVER 5
(mult 8 + 2 sts)

☐ = K on RS; P on WS

= Slip 2 sts onto cn and hold in back; K2; K2 from cn

= Slip 2 sts onto cn and hold in front; K2; K2 from cn

Row 7
Row 5
Row 3
Row 1 (RS)

← rep →

End   Beg

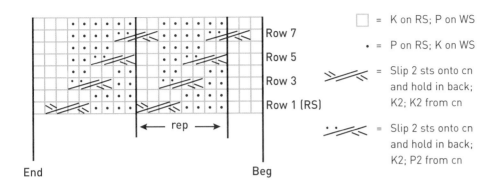

Row 7
Row 5
Row 3
Row 1 (RS)

← rep →

End   Beg

☐ = K on RS; P on WS

• = P on RS; K on WS

= Slip 2 sts onto cn and hold in back; K2; K2 from cn

= Slip 2 sts onto cn and hold in back; K2; P2 from cn

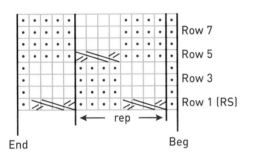

Row 7
Row 5
Row 3
Row 1 (RS)

← rep →

End   Beg

• = P on RS; K on WS

= Slip 2 sts onto cn and hold in front; K2; K2 from cn

☐ = K on RS; P on WS

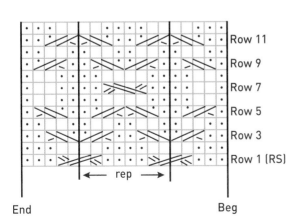

Row 11
Row 9
Row 7
Row 5
Row 3
Row 1 (RS)

← rep →

End   Beg

• = P on RS; K on WS

= Slip 2 sts onto cn and hold in back; K2; K2 from cn

☐ = K on RS; P on WS

= Slip next st onto cn and hold in back; K2; P1 from cn

= Slip 2 sts onto cn and hold in front; P1; K2 from cn

= Slip 2 sts onto cn and hold in front; K2; K2 from cn

ALLOVER 9
(mult 8 + 10 sts)

• = P on RS; K on WS

☐ = K on RS; P on WS

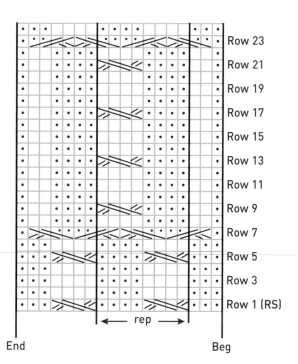 = Slip 2 sts onto cn and hold in front; K2; K2 from cn

= Slip 2 sts onto cn and hold in front; P2; K2 from cn

= Slip 2 sts onto cn and hold in back; K2; P2 from cn

= Slip 2 sts onto cn and hold in back; K2; K2 from cn

Row 15
Row 13
Row 11
Row 9
Row 7
Row 5
Row 3
Row 1 (RS)

← rep →

End   Beg

ALLOVER 10
(mult 8 + 10 sts)

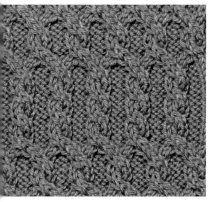

• = P on RS; K on WS

= Slip 2 sts onto cn and hold in front; K2; K2 from cn

☐ = K on RS; P on WS

= Slip 2 sts onto cn and hold in back; K2; P2 from cn

= Slip 2 sts onto cn and hold in front; P2; K2 from cn

Row 23
Row 21
Row 19
Row 17
Row 15
Row 13
Row 11
Row 9
Row 7
Row 5
Row 3
Row 1 (RS)

← rep →

End   Beg

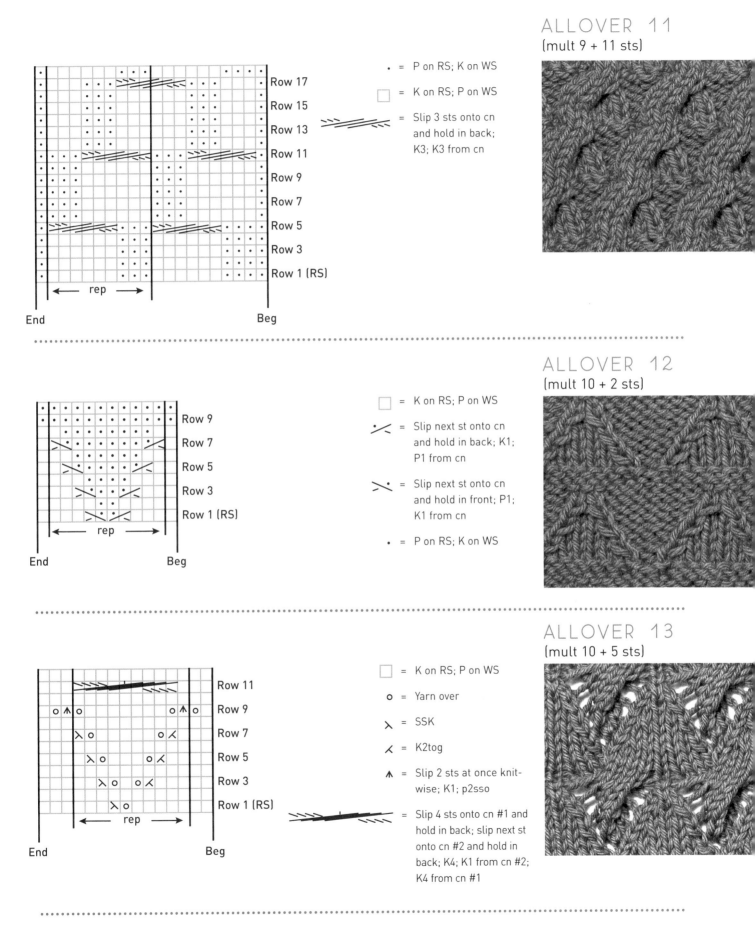

ALLOVER 11
(mult 9 + 11 sts)

Row 17
Row 15
Row 13
Row 11
Row 9
Row 7
Row 5
Row 3
Row 1 (RS)

rep

End   Beg

• = P on RS; K on WS

☐ = K on RS; P on WS

= Slip 3 sts onto cn and hold in back; K3; K3 from cn

ALLOVER 12
(mult 10 + 2 sts)

Row 9
Row 7
Row 5
Row 3
Row 1 (RS)

rep

End   Beg

☐ = K on RS; P on WS

= Slip next st onto cn and hold in back; K1; P1 from cn

= Slip next st onto cn and hold in front; P1; K1 from cn

• = P on RS; K on WS

ALLOVER 13
(mult 10 + 5 sts)

Row 11
Row 9
Row 7
Row 5
Row 3
Row 1 (RS)

rep

End   Beg

☐ = K on RS; P on WS

o = Yarn over

⅄ = SSK

⅄ = K2tog

⋀ = Slip 2 sts at once knitwise; K1; p2sso

= Slip 4 sts onto cn #1 and hold in back; slip next st onto cn #2 and hold in back; K4; K1 from cn #2; K4 from cn #1

ALLOVER 14
(mult 11 + 1 sts)

• = P on RS; K on WS

☐ = K on RS; P on WS

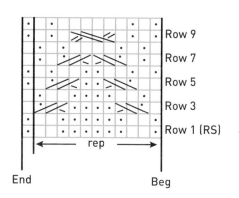

= Slip 2 sts onto cn and hold in front; P1; K2 from cn

= Slip next st onto cn and hold in back; K2; P1 from cn

= Slip 2 sts onto cn and hold in front; K2; K2 from cn

Row 9
Row 7
Row 5
Row 3
Row 1 (RS)

End ← rep → Beg

ALLOVER 15
(mult 12 + 2 sts)

☐ = K on RS; P on WS

= Slip 4 sts onto cn and hold in back; K4; K4 from cn

= Slip 4 sts onto cn and hold in front; K4; K4 from cn

Note: Work dark-colored squares with Color A; work light-colored squares with Color B.

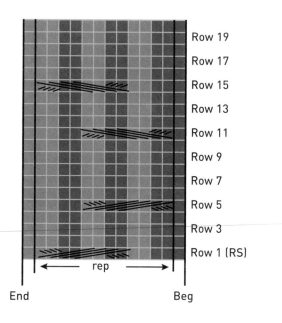

Row 19
Row 17
Row 15
Row 13
Row 11
Row 9
Row 7
Row 5
Row 3
Row 1 (RS)

End ← rep → Beg

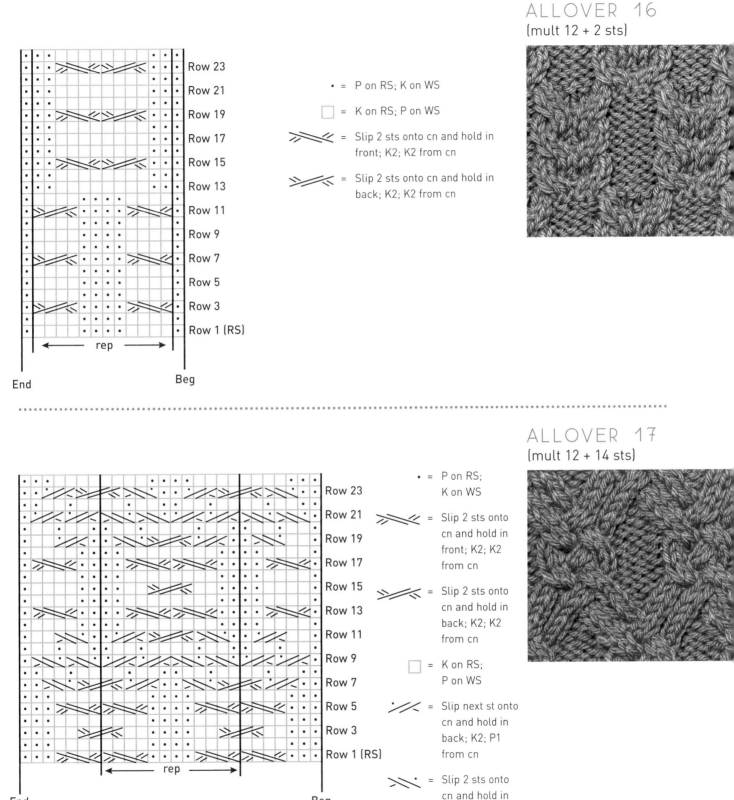

ALLOVER 16
(mult 12 + 2 sts)

Row 23
Row 21
Row 19
Row 17
Row 15
Row 13
Row 11
Row 9
Row 7
Row 5
Row 3
Row 1 (RS)

rep

End   Beg

• = P on RS; K on WS

☐ = K on RS; P on WS

= Slip 2 sts onto cn and hold in front; K2; K2 from cn

= Slip 2 sts onto cn and hold in back; K2; K2 from cn

ALLOVER 17
(mult 12 + 14 sts)

Row 23
Row 21
Row 19
Row 17
Row 15
Row 13
Row 11
Row 9
Row 7
Row 5
Row 3
Row 1 (RS)

rep

End   Beg

• = P on RS; K on WS

= Slip 2 sts onto cn and hold in front; K2; K2 from cn

= Slip 2 sts onto cn and hold in back; K2; K2 from cn

☐ = K on RS; P on WS

= Slip next st onto cn and hold in back; K2; P1 from cn

= Slip 2 sts onto cn and hold in front; P1; K2 from cn

ALLOVER 18
(mult 12 + 6 sts)

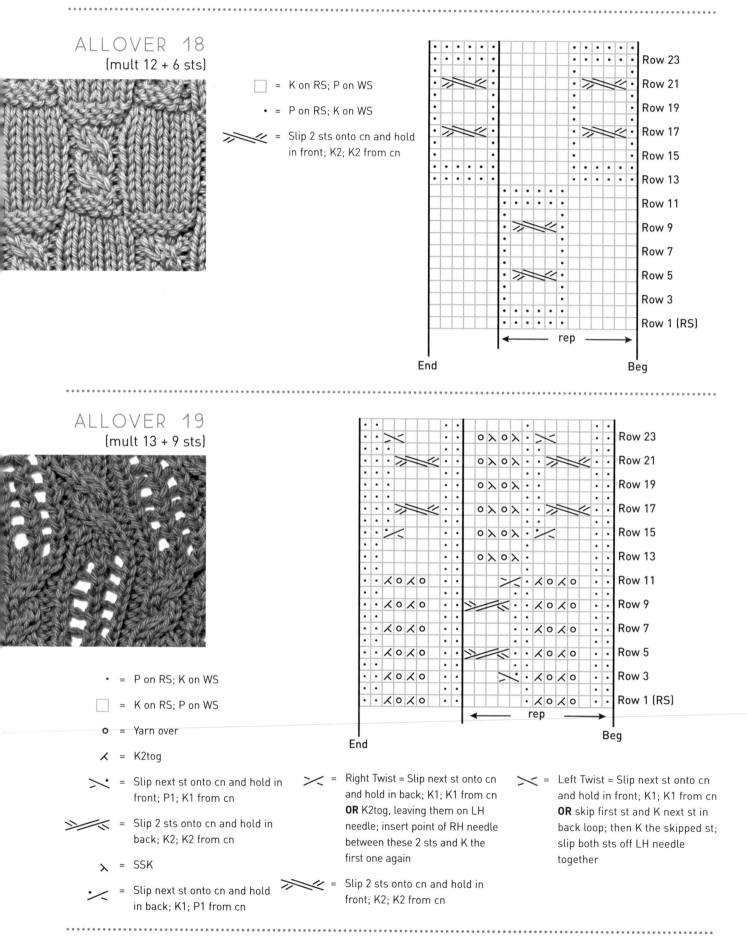

□ = K on RS; P on WS

• = P on RS; K on WS

= Slip 2 sts onto cn and hold in front; K2; K2 from cn

Row 23
Row 21
Row 19
Row 17
Row 15
Row 13
Row 11
Row 9
Row 7
Row 5
Row 3
Row 1 (RS)

←— rep —→

End   Beg

ALLOVER 19
(mult 13 + 9 sts)

Row 23
Row 21
Row 19
Row 17
Row 15
Row 13
Row 11
Row 9
Row 7
Row 5
Row 3
Row 1 (RS)

←— rep —→

End   Beg

• = P on RS; K on WS

□ = K on RS; P on WS

o = Yarn over

⋏ = K2tog

= Slip next st onto cn and hold in front; P1; K1 from cn

= Slip 2 sts onto cn and hold in back; K2; K2 from cn

⋋ = SSK

= Slip next st onto cn and hold in back; K1; P1 from cn

= Right Twist = Slip next st onto cn and hold in back; K1; K1 from cn **OR** K2tog, leaving them on LH needle; insert point of RH needle between these 2 sts and K the first one again

= Slip 2 sts onto cn and hold in front; K2; K2 from cn

= Left Twist = Slip next st onto cn and hold in front; K1; K1 from cn **OR** skip first st and K next st in back loop; then K the skipped st; slip both sts off LH needle together

164

ALLOVER 20
(mult 14 + 2 sts)

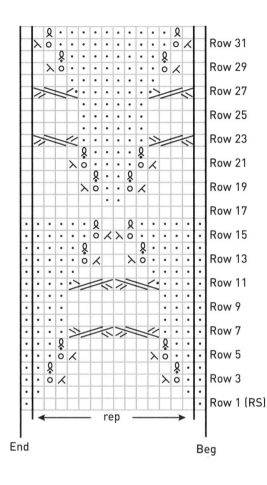

Row 31
Row 29
Row 27
Row 25
Row 23
Row 21
Row 19
Row 17
Row 15
Row 13
Row 11
Row 9
Row 7
Row 5
Row 3
Row 1 (RS)

rep

End   Beg

• = P on RS; K on WS

☐ = K on RS; P on WS

o = Yarn over

⅄ = SSK

⋏ = K2tog

ᛘ = K through back loop on WS

⟩⟩ = Slip 2 sts onto cn and hold in front; K2; K2 from cn

⟩⟩ = Slip 2 sts onto cn and hold in back; K2; K2 from cn

⟩⟩ = Slip 2 sts onto cn and hold in front; P1, K1; K2 from cn

⟩⟩ = Slip 2 sts onto cn and hold in back; K2; (K1, P1) from cn

ᛘ = P through back loop on WS

ALLOVER 21
(mult 14 + 14 sts)

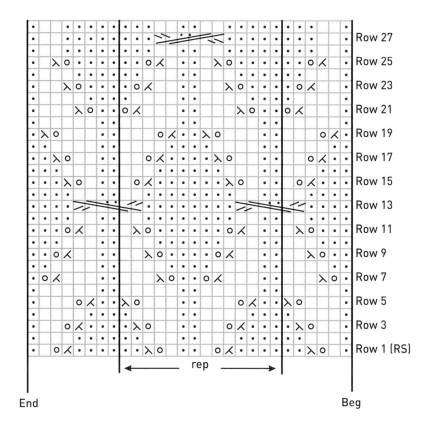

Row 27
Row 25
Row 23
Row 21
Row 19
Row 17
Row 15
Row 13
Row 11
Row 9
Row 7
Row 5
Row 3
Row 1 (RS)

←—— rep ——→

End   Beg

• = P on RS; K on WS

☐ = K on RS; P on WS

o = Yarn over

⋋ = SSK

⋌ = K2tog

= Slip 2 sts onto cn #1 and hold in front; slip next 2 sts onto cn #2 and hold in back; K2; P2 from cn #2; K2 from cn #1

= Slip 2 sts onto cn #1 and hold in back; slip next 2 sts onto cn #2 and hold in back; K2; P2 from cn #2; K2 from cn #1

ALLOVER 22
(mult 16 + 2 sts)

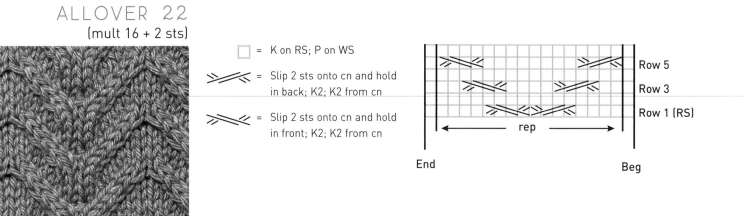

☐ = K on RS; P on WS

= Slip 2 sts onto cn and hold in back; K2; K2 from cn

= Slip 2 sts onto cn and hold in front; K2; K2 from cn

Row 5
Row 3
Row 1 (RS)

←—— rep ——→

End   Beg

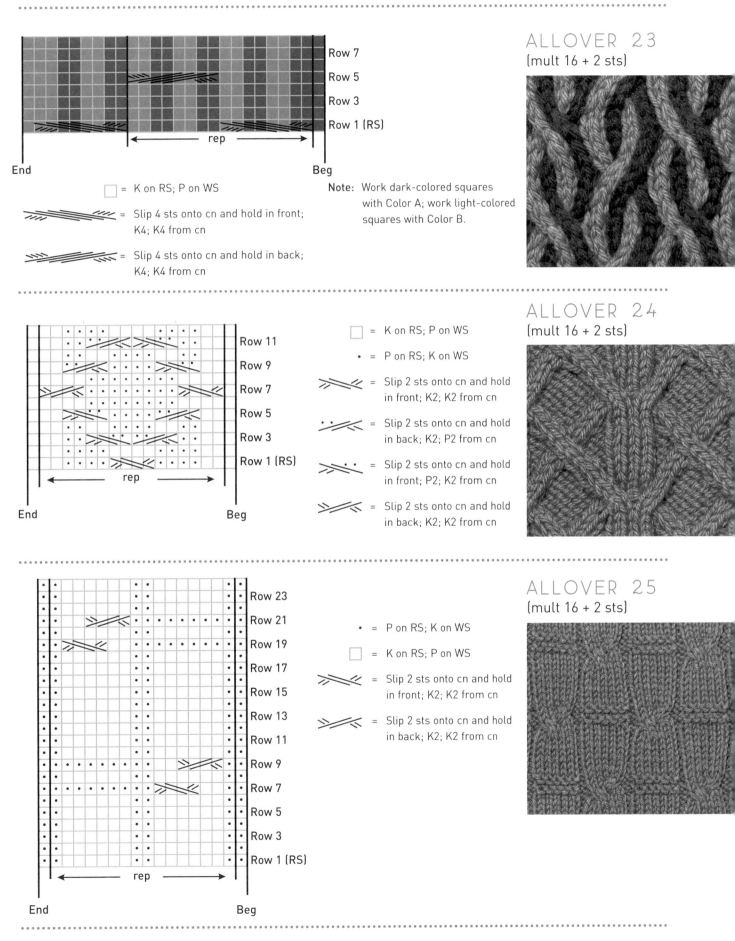

ALLOVER 23
(mult 16 + 2 sts)

Row 7
Row 5
Row 3
Row 1 (RS)

← rep →

End   Beg

☐ = K on RS; P on WS

= Slip 4 sts onto cn and hold in front; K4; K4 from cn

= Slip 4 sts onto cn and hold in back; K4; K4 from cn

Note: Work dark-colored squares with Color A; work light-colored squares with Color B.

ALLOVER 24
(mult 16 + 2 sts)

Row 11
Row 9
Row 7
Row 5
Row 3
Row 1 (RS)

← rep →

End   Beg

☐ = K on RS; P on WS

• = P on RS; K on WS

= Slip 2 sts onto cn and hold in front; K2; K2 from cn

= Slip 2 sts onto cn and hold in back; K2; P2 from cn

= Slip 2 sts onto cn and hold in front; P2; K2 from cn

= Slip 2 sts onto cn and hold in back; K2; K2 from cn

ALLOVER 25
(mult 16 + 2 sts)

Row 23
Row 21
Row 19
Row 17
Row 15
Row 13
Row 11
Row 9
Row 7
Row 5
Row 3
Row 1 (RS)

← rep →

End   Beg

• = P on RS; K on WS

☐ = K on RS; P on WS

= Slip 2 sts onto cn and hold in front; K2; K2 from cn

= Slip 2 sts onto cn and hold in back; K2; K2 from cn

ALLOVER 26
(mult 16 + 14 sts)

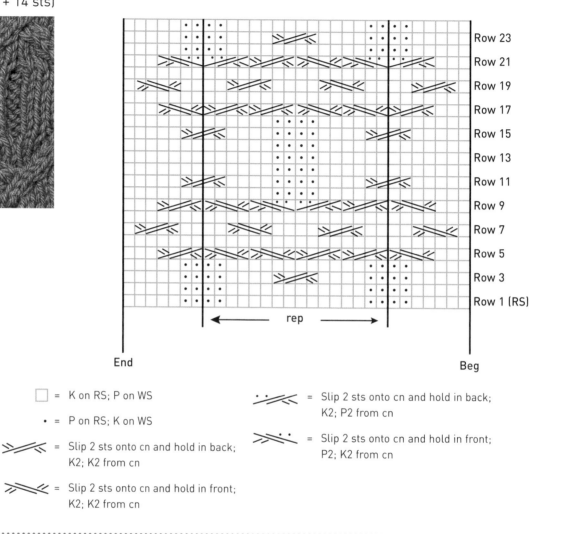

Row 23
Row 21
Row 19
Row 17
Row 15
Row 13
Row 11
Row 9
Row 7
Row 5
Row 3
Row 1 (RS)

← rep →

End   Beg

☐ = K on RS; P on WS

• = P on RS; K on WS

= Slip 2 sts onto cn and hold in back;
K2; K2 from cn

= Slip 2 sts onto cn and hold in front;
K2; K2 from cn

= Slip 2 sts onto cn and hold in back;
K2; P2 from cn

= Slip 2 sts onto cn and hold in front;
P2; K2 from cn

ALLOVER 27
(mult 18 + 2 sts)

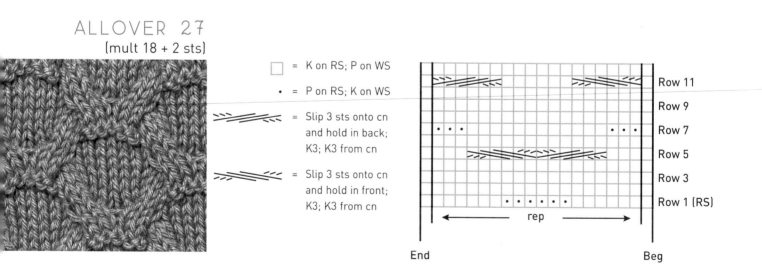

☐ = K on RS; P on WS

• = P on RS; K on WS

= Slip 3 sts onto cn
and hold in back;
K3; K3 from cn

= Slip 3 sts onto cn
and hold in front;
K3; K3 from cn

Row 11
Row 9
Row 7
Row 5
Row 3
Row 1 (RS)

← rep →

End   Beg

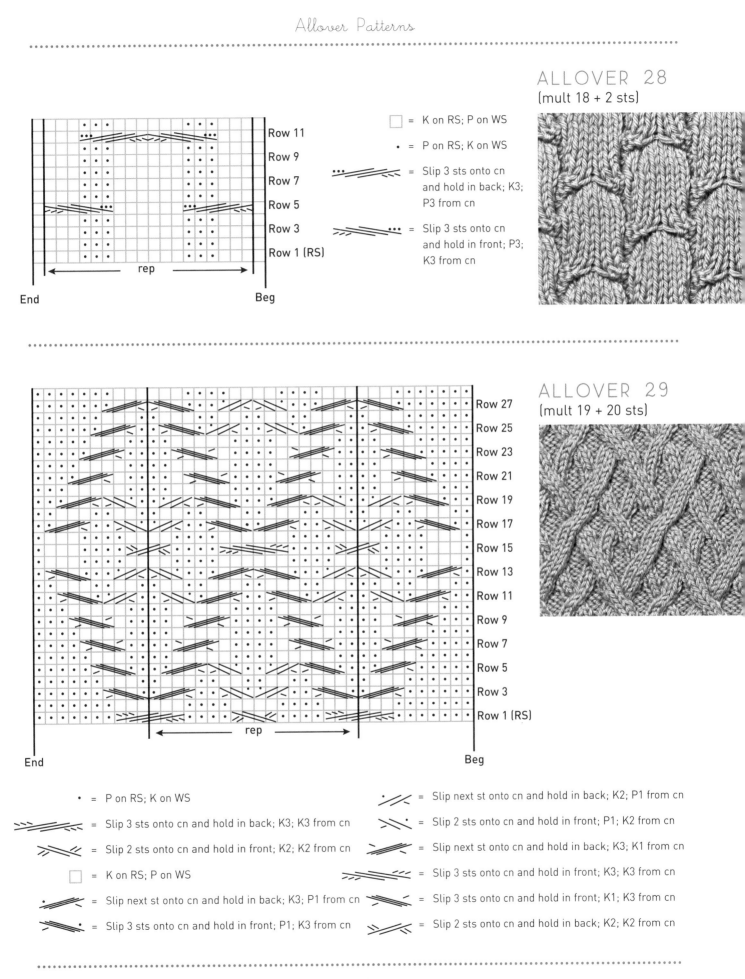

ALLOVER 28
(mult 18 + 2 sts)

Row 11
Row 9
Row 7
Row 5
Row 3
Row 1 (RS)

rep

End   Beg

☐ = K on RS; P on WS

• = P on RS; K on WS

= Slip 3 sts onto cn and hold in back; K3; P3 from cn

= Slip 3 sts onto cn and hold in front; P3; K3 from cn

ALLOVER 29
(mult 19 + 20 sts)

Row 27
Row 25
Row 23
Row 21
Row 19
Row 17
Row 15
Row 13
Row 11
Row 9
Row 7
Row 5
Row 3
Row 1 (RS)

rep

End   Beg

• = P on RS; K on WS

= Slip 3 sts onto cn and hold in back; K3; K3 from cn

= Slip 2 sts onto cn and hold in front; K2; K2 from cn

☐ = K on RS; P on WS

= Slip next st onto cn and hold in back; K3; P1 from cn

= Slip 3 sts onto cn and hold in front; P1; K3 from cn

= Slip next st onto cn and hold in back; K2; P1 from cn

= Slip 2 sts onto cn and hold in front; P1; K2 from cn

= Slip next st onto cn and hold in back; K3; K1 from cn

= Slip 3 sts onto cn and hold in front; K3; K3 from cn

= Slip 3 sts onto cn and hold in front; K1; K3 from cn

= Slip 2 sts onto cn and hold in back; K2; K2 from cn

ALLOVER 30
(mult 20 + 20 sts)

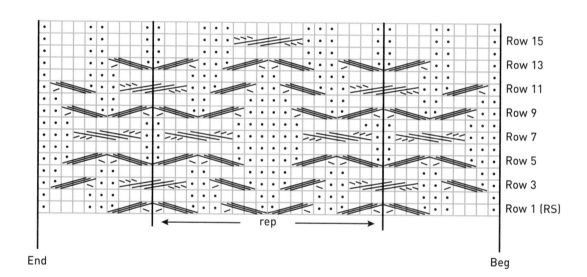

- • = P on RS; K on WS

- ☐ = K on RS; P on WS

- ⧄ = Slip 3 sts onto cn and hold in front; P1; K3 from cn

- ⧄ = Slip next st onto cn and hold in back; K3; P1 from cn

- ⧄ = Slip 3 sts onto cn and hold in back; K3; K3 from cn

- ⧄ = Slip 3 sts onto cn and hold in front; K3; K3 from cn

Row 15
Row 13
Row 11
Row 9
Row 7
Row 5
Row 3
Row 1 (RS)

← rep →

End

Beg

ALLOVER 31
(mult 20 + 22 sts)

= P on RS; K on WS

= K on RS; P on WS

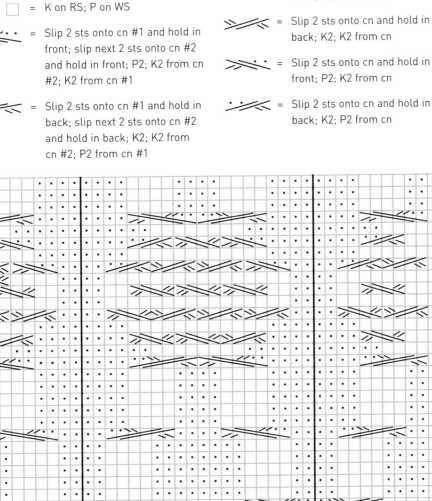

= Slip 2 sts onto cn #1 and hold in front; slip next 2 sts onto cn #2 and hold in front; P2; K2 from cn #2; K2 from cn #1

= Slip 2 sts onto cn #1 and hold in back; slip next 2 sts onto cn #2 and hold in back; K2; K2 from cn #2; P2 from cn #1

= Slip 2 sts onto cn and hold in front; K2; K2 from cn

= Slip 2 sts onto cn and hold in back; K2; K2 from cn

= Slip 2 sts onto cn and hold in front; P2; K2 from cn

= Slip 2 sts onto cn and hold in back; K2; P2 from cn

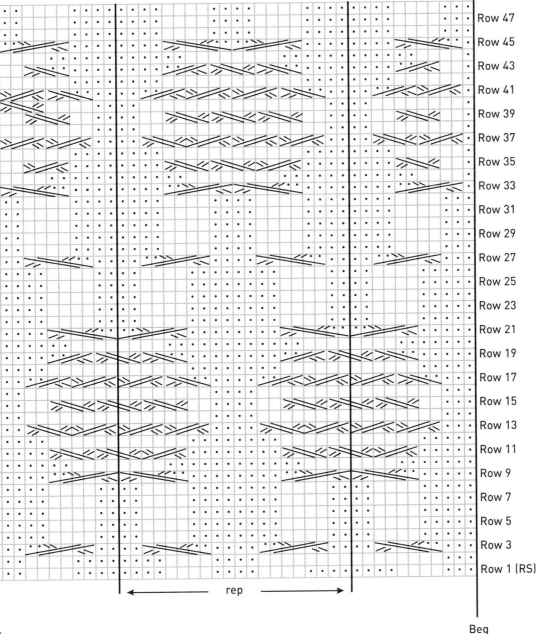

Row 47
Row 45
Row 43
Row 41
Row 39
Row 37
Row 35
Row 33
Row 31
Row 29
Row 27
Row 25
Row 23
Row 21
Row 19
Row 17
Row 15
Row 13
Row 11
Row 9
Row 7
Row 5
Row 3
Row 1 (RS)

← rep →

End

Beg

171

ALLOVER 32

(mult 22 + 19 sts, inc to
mult 26 + 23 sts)

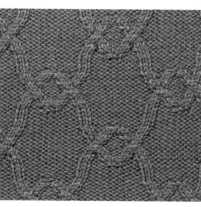

• = P on RS; K on WS

☐ = K on RS; P on WS

⬛ = No stitch

M = M1 = Insert LH needle under the horizontal strand between two sts from front to back and K it through back loop

⋎ = Central Double Increase = (Increases from 1 st to 3 sts) = K into back and then into front of indicated st and slip them off LH needle onto RH needle; insert point of LH needle behind the vertical strand that runs downward between the two sts just made, and K *into the front* of it

⟋⟍• = Slip 2 sts onto cn and hold in front; P1; K2 from cn

⟋⟍ = Slip next st onto cn and hold in back; K2; P1 from cn

⟋⟍ = Slip 2 sts onto cn and hold in front; K2; K2 from cn

⟑₅ = (Decreases from 5 sts to 1 st) = Slip next 3 sts with yarn in back, drop yarn; *pass the second st on RH needle over the first st on RH needle; slip first st from RH needle back to LH needle; pass the second st on LH needle over the first st on LH needle; **slip first st from LH needle back to RH needle and repeat from * to ** once again; pick up yarn and K remaining st

⟍⟋ = Slip 2 sts onto cn and hold in back; K2; K2 from cn

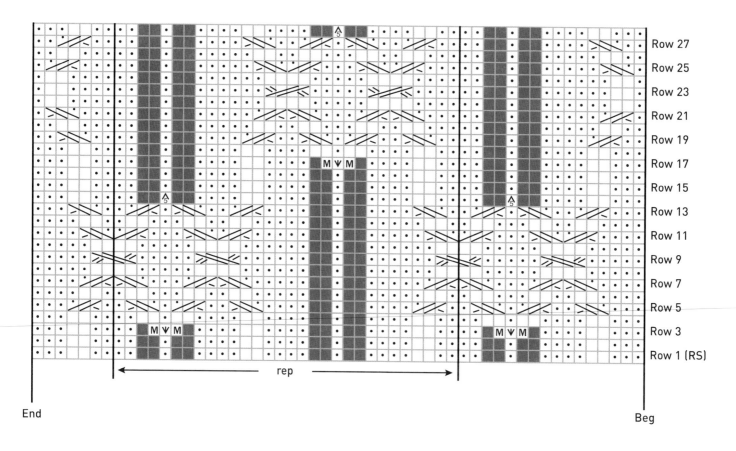

Row 27
Row 25
Row 23
Row 21
Row 19
Row 17
Row 15
Row 13
Row 11
Row 9
Row 7
Row 5
Row 3
Row 1 (RS)

⟵ rep ⟶

End

Beg

ALLOVER 33
(mult 24 + 12 sts)

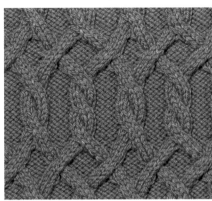

- • = P on RS; K on WS

- ☐ = K on RS; P on WS

-  = Slip 3 sts onto cn and hold in front; K3; K3 from cn

- = Slip 2 sts onto cn and hold in back; K3; P2 from cn

- = Slip 3 sts onto cn and hold in front; P2; K3 from cn

- = Slip 3 sts onto cn and hold in back; K3; K3 from cn

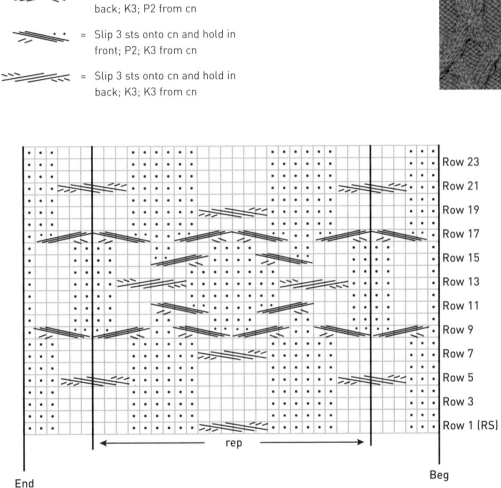

Row 23
Row 21
Row 19
Row 17
Row 15
Row 13
Row 11
Row 9
Row 7
Row 5
Row 3
Row 1 (RS)

rep

End   Beg

ALLOVER 34
(mult 24 + 26 sts)

- • = P on RS; K on WS

- 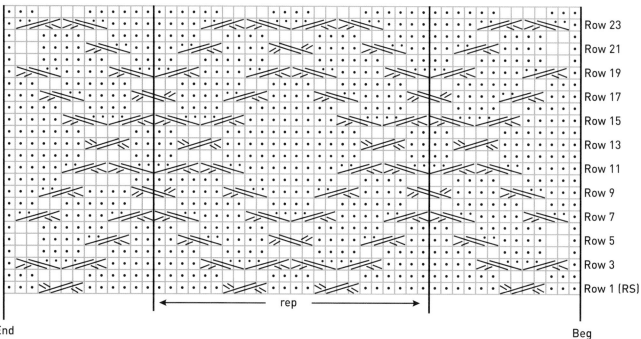 = Slip 2 sts onto cn and hold in back; K2; K2 from cn

- □ = K on RS; P on WS

- = Slip 2 sts onto cn and hold in back; K2; P2 from cn

- = Slip 2 sts onto cn and hold in front; P2; K2 from cn

- = Slip 2 sts onto cn and hold in front; K2; K2 from cn

Row 23
Row 21
Row 19
Row 17
Row 15
Row 13
Row 11
Row 9
Row 7
Row 5
Row 3
Row 1 (RS)

← rep →

End

Beg

□ = K on RS; P on WS

• = P on RS; K on WS

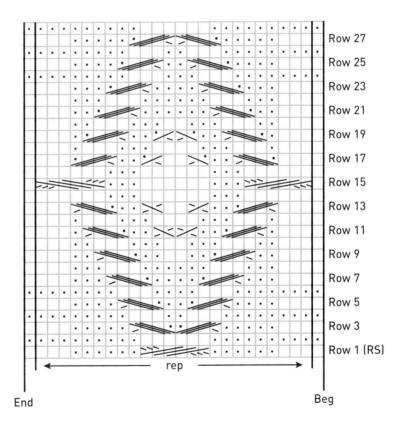 = Slip 3 sts onto cn and hold in back; K3; K3 from cn

= Slip next st onto cn and hold in back; K3; P1 from cn

= Slip 3 sts onto cn and hold in front; P1; K3 from cn

>< = Right Twist = Slip next st onto cn and hold in back; K1; K1 from cn **OR** K2tog, leaving them on LH needle; insert point of RH needle between these 2 sts and K the first one again

>< = Left Twist = Slip next st onto cn and hold in front; K1; K1 from cn **OR** skip first st and K next st *in back loop*; then K the skipped st; slip both sts off LH needle together

= Slip 3 sts onto cn and hold in front; K3; K3 from cn

>< = Slip next st onto cn and hold in front; P1; K1 from cn

>< = Slip next st onto cn and hold in back; K1; P1 from cn

Row 27
Row 25
Row 23
Row 21
Row 19
Row 17
Row 15
Row 13
Row 11
Row 9
Row 7
Row 5
Row 3
Row 1 (RS)

⟵ rep ⟶

End   Beg

ALLOVER 36
(4-st panel)

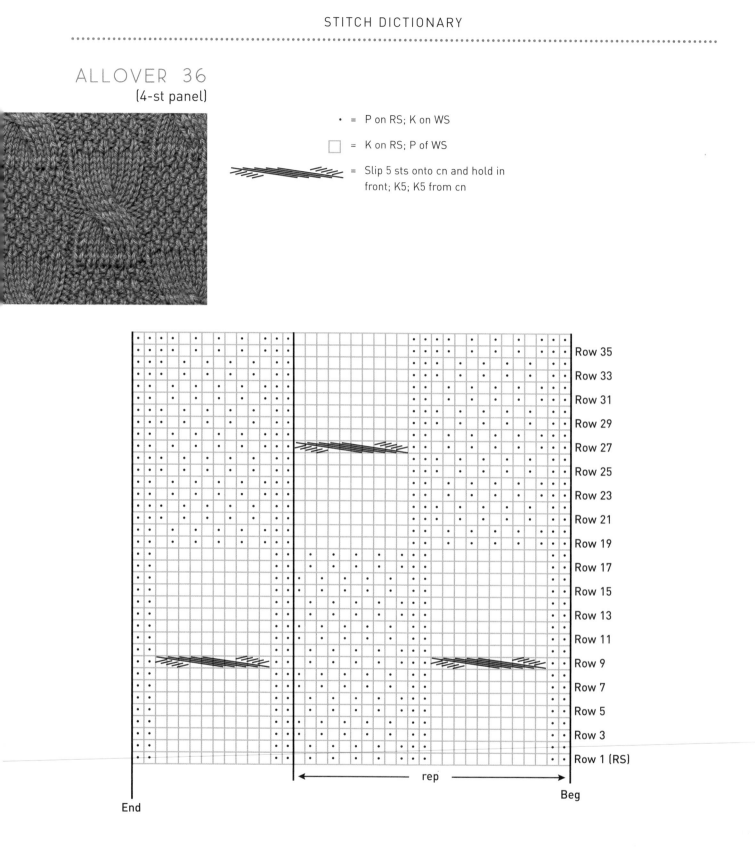

- • = P on RS; K on WS

- ☐ = K on RS; P of WS

- ⬎ = Slip 5 sts onto cn and hold in front; K5; K5 from cn

Row 35
Row 33
Row 31
Row 29
Row 27
Row 25
Row 23
Row 21
Row 19
Row 17
Row 15
Row 13
Row 11
Row 9
Row 7
Row 5
Row 3
Row 1 (RS)

⟵ rep ⟶

End

Beg

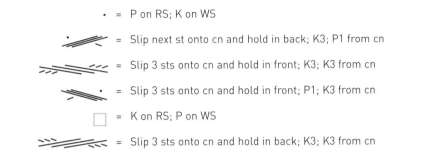

• = P on RS; K on WS

= Slip next st onto cn and hold in back; K3; P1 from cn

= Slip 3 sts onto cn and hold in front; K3; K3 from cn

= Slip 3 sts onto cn and hold in front; P1; K3 from cn

☐ = K on RS; P on WS

= Slip 3 sts onto cn and hold in back; K3; K3 from cn

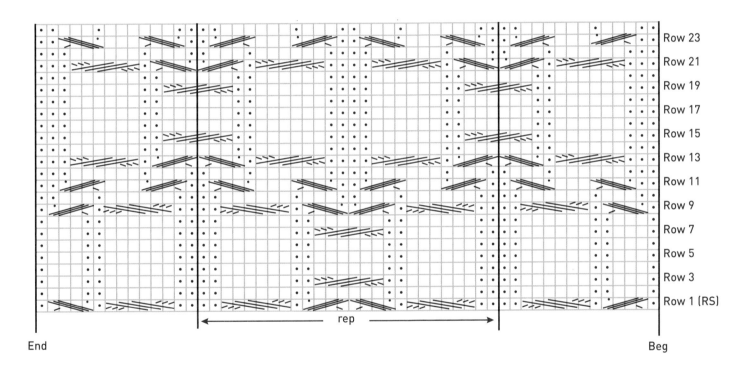

Row 23
Row 21
Row 19
Row 17
Row 15
Row 13
Row 11
Row 9
Row 7
Row 5
Row 3
Row 1 (RS)

rep

End

Beg

ALLOVER 38
(mult 26 + 22 sts)

• = P on RS; K on WS

= Slip 2 sts onto cn and hold in back; K2; K2 from cn

□ = K on RS; P on WS

= Slip next st onto cn and hold in back; K2; P1 from cn

= Slip 2 sts onto cn and hold in front; P1; K2 from cn

= Slip 2 sts onto cn and hold in front; K2; K2 from cn

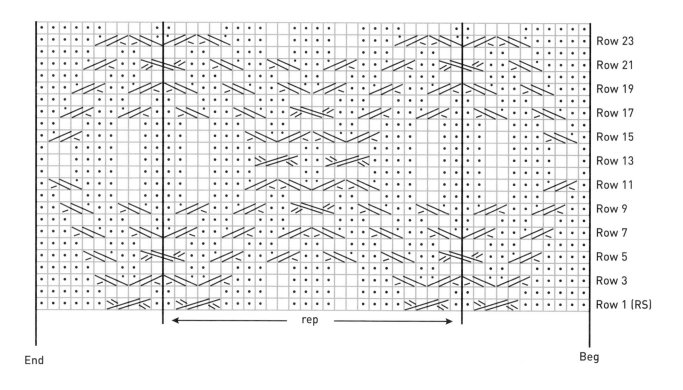

Row 23
Row 21
Row 19
Row 17
Row 15
Row 13
Row 11
Row 9
Row 7
Row 5
Row 3
Row 1 (RS)

rep

End

Beg

• = P on RS; K on WS

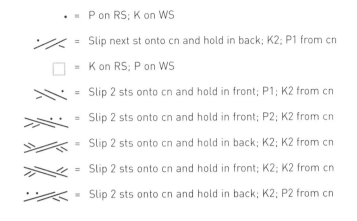

= Slip next st onto cn and hold in back; K2; P1 from cn

☐ = K on RS; P on WS

= Slip 2 sts onto cn and hold in front; P1; K2 from cn

= Slip 2 sts onto cn and hold in front; P2; K2 from cn

= Slip 2 sts onto cn and hold in back; K2; K2 from cn

= Slip 2 sts onto cn and hold in front; K2; K2 from cn

= Slip 2 sts onto cn and hold in back; K2; P2 from cn

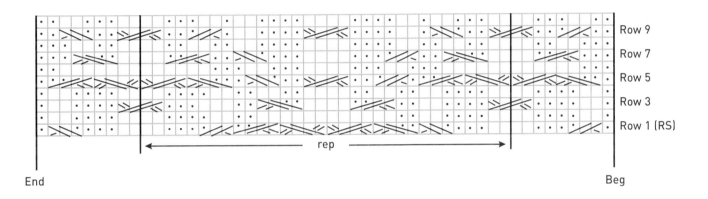

Row 9

Row 7

Row 5

Row 3

Row 1 (RS)

rep

End

Beg

ALLOVER 40
(mult 32 + 32 sts)

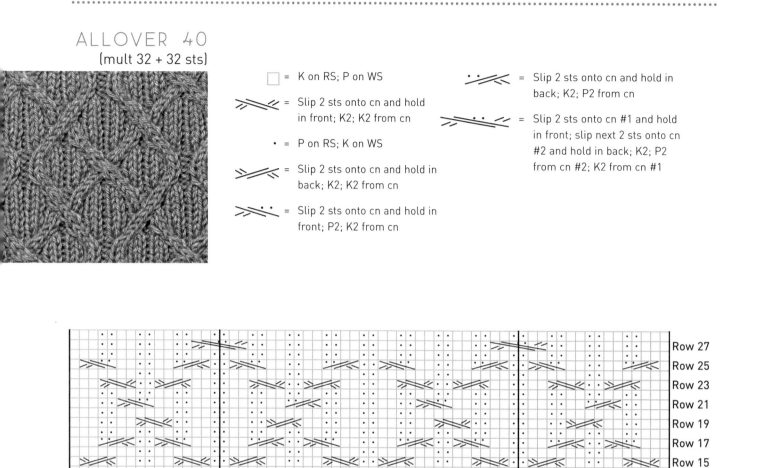

☐ = K on RS; P on WS

= Slip 2 sts onto cn and hold in front; K2; K2 from cn

• = P on RS; K on WS

= Slip 2 sts onto cn and hold in back; K2; K2 from cn

= Slip 2 sts onto cn and hold in front; P2; K2 from cn

= Slip 2 sts onto cn and hold in back; K2; P2 from cn

= Slip 2 sts onto cn #1 and hold in front; slip next 2 sts onto cn #2 and hold in back; K2; P2 from cn #2; K2 from cn #1

Row 27
Row 25
Row 23
Row 21
Row 19
Row 17
Row 15
Row 13
Row 11
Row 9
Row 7
Row 5
Row 3
Row 1 (RS)

← rep →

End

Beg

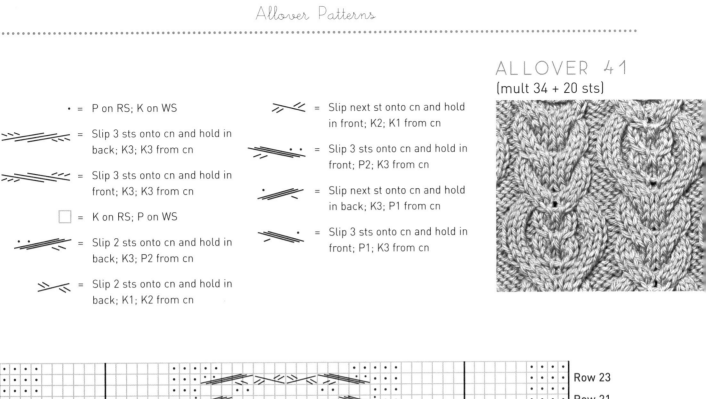

ALLOVER 41
(mult 34 + 20 sts)

Legend:

- • = P on RS; K on WS
- = Slip 3 sts onto cn and hold in back; K3; K3 from cn
- = Slip 3 sts onto cn and hold in front; K3; K3 from cn
- □ = K on RS; P on WS
- = Slip 2 sts onto cn and hold in back; K3; P2 from cn
- = Slip 2 sts onto cn and hold in back; K1; K2 from cn
- = Slip next st onto cn and hold in front; K2; K1 from cn
- = Slip 3 sts onto cn and hold in front; P2; K3 from cn
- = Slip next st onto cn and hold in back; K3; P1 from cn
- = Slip 3 sts onto cn and hold in front; P1; K3 from cn

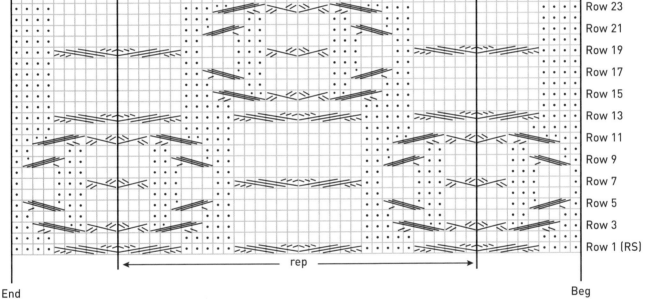

Row 23
Row 21
Row 19
Row 17
Row 15
Row 13
Row 11
Row 9
Row 7
Row 5
Row 3
Row 1 (RS)

← rep →

End

Beg

ALLOVER 42
(mult 34 + 36 sts)

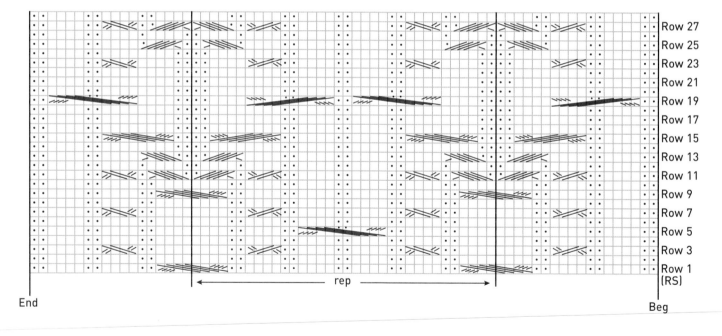

• = P on RS; K on WS

☐ = K on RS; P on WS

= Slip 4 sts onto cn and hold in front; K4; K4 from cn

= Slip 2 sts onto cn and hold in back; K2; K2 from cn

= Slip 2 sts onto cn and hold in front; K2; K2 from cn

= Slip next 4 sts onto cn #1 and hold in front; slip next 2 sts onto cn #2 and hold in back; K4; P2 from cn #2; K4 from cn #1

= Slip next st onto cn and hold in back; K4; P1 from cn

= Slip 4 sts onto cn and hold in front; P1; K4 from cn

= Slip 4 sts onto cn and hold in back; K4; K4 from cn

= Slip 4 sts onto cn #1 and hold in back; slip next 2 sts onto cn #2 and hold in back; K4; P2 from cn #2; K4 from cn #1

Row 27
Row 25
Row 23
Row 21
Row 19
Row 17
Row 15
Row 13
Row 11
Row 9
Row 7
Row 5
Row 3
Row 1 (RS)

← rep →

End

Beg

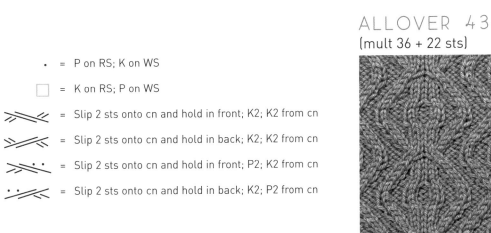

• = P on RS; K on WS

☐ = K on RS; P on WS

= Slip 2 sts onto cn and hold in front; K2; K2 from cn

= Slip 2 sts onto cn and hold in back; K2; K2 from cn

= Slip 2 sts onto cn and hold in front; P2; K2 from cn

= Slip 2 sts onto cn and hold in back; K2; P2 from cn

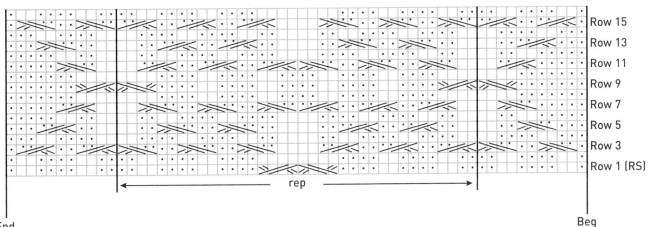

Row 15
Row 13
Row 11
Row 9
Row 7
Row 5
Row 3
Row 1 (RS)

rep

End

Beg

RESOURCES

In this section, you'll find information on yarn choice and yarn
substitution and materials suppliers, as well as an index—everything
you need to enjoy cable knitting.

Yarn Choice and Substitution

All yarns possess characteristics that will affect the way the yarn appears and behaves when knitted. The projects in this book were designed for a specific yarn. In order to duplicate the sweaters as photographed, I suggest that you use the designated yarns.

However, if you would like to make a yarn substitution, be sure to choose one of similar weight to the one called for in the pattern. Yarn sizes and weights are usually located on the label, but for an accurate test, knit a swatch of Stockinette Stitch Pattern (see instructions below) using the recommended needle size, making it at least 4" square.

Stockinette St Pattern (any number of sts)
Row 1 (RS): Knit across.

Row 2: Purl across.

Repeat Rows 1 and 2 for patt.

Count the number of stitches over 4" and refer to the table below to determine its weight.

The fabric should also be similar in drape, texture, and appearance. Since the amount per skein varies, be sure to base substitution on the total yardage called for rather than the number of skeins.

YARN SIZE	YARN WEIGHT	STITCHES PER 4" IN STOCKINETTE STITCH
(1)	Super Fine (Fingering weight)	27 or more
(2)	Fine (Sport weight)	23–26 sts
(3)	Light (DK weight)	21–24 sts
(4)	Medium (Worsted weight)	16–20 sts
(5)	Bulky (Bulky weight)	12–15 sts
(6)	Super Bulky (Super Bulky weight)	11 or fewer

Material Resources

MANUFACTURERS

The yarns used in this book are widely available at fine yarn stores everywhere. We've offered this guide as a resource for locating the store nearest you. Each of the websites listed, unless otherwise noted, offers a store locator to make it easy to find the yarn you want quickly and easily. Many of the websites will also allow you to place on-line orders.

AURORA YARNS
P.O. Box 3068
Moss Beach, CA 94038
(650) 728-8554
www.garnstudio.com

BLUE SKY ALPACAS
2831 199th Avenue NW
P.O. Box 387
Cedar, MN 55011
(763) 753-5815
www.blueskyalpacas.com

CASCADE YARNS
1224 Andover Park East
Tukwila, WA 98188
(206) 574-0440
www.cascadeyarns.com

CLASSIC ELITE YARNS
122 Western Avenue
Lowell, MA 01851
(978) 453-2837
www.classiceliteyarns.com

FILATURA DI CROSA
(See Tahki/Stacy Charles)

GARNSTUDIO
(see Aurora Yarns)

GGH
(see Muench Yarns)

HARRISVILLE DESIGNS
P.O. Box 806
Harrisville, NH 03450
(603) 827-3333
www.harrisville.com

JAEGER YARNS
(see Westminster Fibers)

JCA, INC.
35 Scales Lane
Townsend, MA 01469
(978) 597-8794
www.jcacrafts.com

Note: JCA Yarns are distributed nationwide. E-mail or call the number listed for suggested retailers. JCA yarns are also available from the Wool Connection listed on page 188.

JHB INTERNATIONAL, INC.
1955 South Quince Street
Denver, CO 80231
(303) 751-8100
www.buttons.com

JUDI & CO.
18 Gallatin Drive
Dix Hills, NY 11746
(631) 499-8480
www.judiandco.com

MUENCH YARNS
1323 Scott Street
Petaluma, CA 94954
(707) 763-9377
www.muenchyarns.com

Material Resources

NORWEGIAN SPIRIT, INC.
N27 W23713 Paul Road, Suite G
Pewaukee, WI 53072
(262) 347-0809
www.spirit-norway.com

ORNAGHI FILATI
(see Aurora Yarns)

PATONS YARNS
320 Livingstone Avenue South
Listowel, Ontario N4W 3H3 Canada
(519) 291-3780
www.patonsyarns.com

PLYMOUTH YARN COMPANY
500 Lafayette Street
P.O. Box 28
Bristol, PA 19007
(215) 788-0459
www.plymouthyarn.com

REYNOLDS YARN
(see JCA, Inc.)

ROWAN YARNS
(see Westminster Fibers)

SKACEL COLLECTION, INC.
P.O. Box 88110
Seattle, WA 98168
(253) 854-2710
www.skacelknitting.com

TAHKI/STACY CHARLES
70-30 80th Street
Ridgewood, NY 11385
(718) 326-4433
www.tahkistacycharles.com

WESTMINSTER FIBERS
4 Townsend West, Suite #8
Nashua, NH 03063
(603) 886-5041
www.knitrowan.com

MAIL ORDER AND INTERNET YARN SOURCES

I always recommend that you visit your local yarn shop whenever you need tools and supplies for a knitting project. If they don't have what you need, try one of the following sources:

PATTERNWORKS
Route 25
P.O. Box 1618
Center Harbor, NH 03226
(800) 438-5464
www.patternworks.com

WOOL CONNECTION
34 East Main Street
Avon, CT 06001
(800) 933-9665
www.woolconnection.com

THE KNITTING GUILD ASSOCIATION

To meet other knitters and to learn more about the craft, contact:

THE KNITTING GUILD ASSOCIATION
1100-H Brandywine Boulevard
Zanesville, OH 43701-7303
(877) 852-9190
E-mail: tkga@tkga.com
Website: www.tkga.com

Index

Index

Acknowledgments

I'm grateful to the following knitters who helped knit samples for this book: Jan Ballew, Helen Borga, Papatya Curtis, Lynn Gates, Gwen Gotsch, Cindy Grosch, Patti Hathaway, Tom Jensen, Cheryl Keeley, Jodi Lewanda, Martha Maddox, Bridget Mohr, JoAnn Moss, Joan Murphy, Holly Neiding, Rachel Nissen, Laura Polley, Pam Porter, Shawn Schoonmaker, Judy Seip, Lou Simon, Rusty Slabinski, Norma Jean Sternschein, Scarlet Taylor, Lesley Terschak, Kerstin Usher, and Sereta Vallo.

Many thanks and much credit must go to my superb technical editor, Charlotte "Eagle Eye" Quiggle. Her input and expertise surely made this a better book; her sense of humor kept me a happy, smiling author throughout!

I'm grateful to Cascade Yarn Company for providing every bit of the beautiful yarn used in the Cable Stitch Pattern Dictionary. Their Cascade 220 yarn comes in oodles of colors, is nicely priced with lots of yardage, is wonderful to knit with, and makes knitted cables positively "pop"! Thank you for your generosity.

Special thanks go to Alice Starmore and Barbara Walker, whose extensive work with cables inspired my own exploration of this exciting topic.

Published in the United States by Potter Craft Publishers, an imprint of the Crown Publishing Group, a division of Random House, Inc., New York.
www.crownpublishing.com
www.clarksonpotter.com

POTTER CRAFT and CLARKSON N. POTTER are trademarks, and POTTER and colophon are registered trademarks of Random House, Inc.

Library of Congress Cataloging-in-Publication Data is available.

ISBN 13: 978-1-4000-9745-6
ISBN 10: 1-4000-9745-2

Printed in Singapore

Design: 3+Co. (www.threeandco.com)
Fashion Photography: Alexandra Grablewski
Flat Fabric Photography: Jacob Hand
Technical Illustrations: Judy Love
Charts and Schematic Illustrations: Melissa Leapman
Technical Editor: Charlotte Quiggle

10 9 8 7 6 5 4 3 2 1

First Edition